NE SAVAGE 2000

Elisabeth Ratcliff

First Published 2000

Published by S.J.H. Print

Printed by S.J.H. Print
Milestone House, Angel Bank,
Bitterley, Nr. Ludlow,
Shropshire SY8 3EY.
Telephone: 01584 891040

Text © E. Ratcliff 2000

ISBN 0 9539576 0 8

NEEN SAVAGE 2000

For Andy & Jenny

With all good wishes

Elisabeth Ratcliff

Elisabeth Ratcliff

NEEN SAVAGE PARISH

Foreword

We owe a debt of gratitude to Mrs. Elisabeth Ratcliff for compiling this impressive work. It is the revision of a previous study and represents hours of painstaking research, providing a "snapshot" of village life in Neen Savage in the year 2000. I am confident that whilst this is of great interest to our contemporaries it will gain in significance as we move into the new century and millennium and will be an invaluable and fascinating resource and reference book for future generations.

As you read this work I am sure that you will be impressed by the many community activities which take place in the parish and by detailed attention Elisabeth has given to each house and its occupants. It is an appropriate work to mark the millennium and an example for other country parishes to follow.

Village life will only flourish if we care for it. This is an example of loving care for the inhabitants and homes of Neen Savage and is based on a sound knowledge of the area and its history.

I warmly commend it to you.

Robert A. Horsfield.

The Rectory
Cleobury Mortimer

Robert A. Horsfield.
Rector of Neen Savage
and Prebendary of
Hereford Cathedral.

Preface

When I was asked by the Millennium Committee if I would write this Neen Savage book for 2000, I must admit that I felt somewhat alarmed at the thought of going, once again, through all the historical research that had had to be done for the "Country Parish - Neen Savage in 1981" book, but no - this, I was told, was to be about Neen Savage as it is now in the year 2000. So, it is not, in any way, a historical record, but, I hope, a picture of this Parish as it stands to-day - with all the houses, including, this time, those in Baveney Wood, and all the Parishioners, so that our children's children and their children after them for future generations, will be able to find out where their ancestors were living at this time, how they came to be here from where, and what they were doing, or had done before retirement, as well as where they were born, and where and when they were married; these descendants will also be able to learn about great-uncles and great-aunts of whose very existence they might not even be aware. So that is what this book is all about - a true record of Neen Savage and its people in this year 2000.

I would like to express my thanks - to all the Parishioners who cooperated by filling in their questionnaires and sending their photographs, - to the Millennium Committee Members for collecting some of those questionnaires for me and, particularly, - to Clare Ratcliff and Jane Smith for their indefatigable work in chasing up and gathering so many of those that had got "lost, stolen or strayed"! I am also deeply indebted to Jane Smith for helping me in so many other ways, including making sure the right photos went with the right house. I do apologise, if I have got anything wrong, facts or spelling, either through misreading what was written or not hearing correctly on the phone, and I ask your forgiveness now.

I am very grateful and say thankyou to the Revd. Prebendary Robert Horsfield for his kindness in agreeing to write the Foreword and I would also thank Stuart Harding, of S.J.H. Print, for his undertaking to print this book and his guidance throughout the process. Finally, I thank my husband Eric for all his work on the map and for his patient understanding of all the time I have had to spend on the computer and his sage advice, always readily available when asked for, without all of which this book would have been much harder to write, last but no means least, I thank him for all his time and trouble helping me with the proof reading.

Elisabeth Ratcliff.
Detton Hall. July 2000.

The Parish of Neen Savage

In this, the forty-eighth year of the reign of our most Sovereign Lady, Her Majesty Queen Elizabeth II, the Parish of Neen Savage is probably little changed, (when compared to urban areas), from what it was some 400 years ago, in the reign of Good Queen Bess. Then, as now, Neen Savage would have been predominantly agricultural, perhaps not so crop-productive and certainly with no roads but more trees, some scrubland, and, possibly, wild boars in the woods and sheep on the pasture. Some of the houses built at that time are still standing, as are some of the cottages, and though, of these, many are now greatly altered in appearance, the basic structure of the old cottages can still be seen. Currently there are two Grade 11* and 13 Grade II Listed buildings in the Parish, nine of which are farmhouses of the 16th Century and the others are a barn, a cart shed, one cottage, the Vicarage and the Church.* With the Roman Fort at Wall Town long abandoned and the mediaeval village at Detton quite disappeared, there might well have been a few brick kilns working, as at Woodend and Overwood, and, of course, there were Blacksmith's forges, but it was not until the 18th century that the mills along the River Rea introduced some light industry into this area. However, the Flax Mills did not last that long, the Paper Mill was burnt down in 1885 and the Corn Mill at Detton ceased in 1930, so when, in 1941, the aerial ropeway, bringing Dhustone from the Magpie Quarry to the station at Detton Ford, was dismantled, any industry in the Parish ceased for the rest of the 20th Century except for the Blacksmiths, which, over the years, became the Mechanical Repair Workshops.

Now, at the beginning of the 21st Century, there are plans to bring some light industry back into the Parish. After the closure of the railway, the goods yard had a somewhat chequered period before becoming partly a County Council Depot, partly a parking place for caravans and some of it the property of the Price family, in which to keep their contracting equipment. Now it all belongs to Philip Price and, with the backing of the Parish Council, he has sought Planning Permission for the erection of 9 small units for Light Industry. Permission was granted on condition that the area would be landscaped with screens of bushes and trees, so as to shelter the buildings and to mitigate any noise, and, that a safer entrance to the site should be made; this has already been done by moving the entrance from just above the old railway line to the top of the rise above the wood. It is hoped that the first occupants, Truform, making pressed metal products, mainly for the building industry, will be re-located from Telford, before too long.

For a full list of these properties – See Appendix I

The population numbers have hardly varied, over the centuries, from the number of "souls" recorded as living in the Parish at the time of the Domesday Book to the present day, although, up until sometime in the late 18th Century, two hamlets, - one at Baveney Wood and one at Overwood - and Detton, known as a township with its own Chapel, were all included in the Parish of Neen Savage. Not many new houses seem to have have been built in the 19th Century but in the 20th, the building of new houses seems to have progressed at, roughly, one every ten years (the cottages for the Elan Valley to Birmingham pipe line workers erected in the 1920s, Meadow Bank in 1934, the 10 Council houses in 1948, Melbury in 1957, Lower Baveney, replacing an earlier farmhouse, in 1964, Baveney Bungalow in 1972 and Little Detton in 1983, amongst others) until the last 10 years, which have seen the building of Avelana and Beneliza, Jeff's Cottage considerably enlarged, and the barns at Stone House, Cleobury Lodge, Lower Neen Farm and at Detton Mill, all converted into dwelling houses.

The conversion of these barns is very much a sign of the times It could be said that the 1950s to early 1980s were good times for farmers. (Were they not accused of being "featherbedded"?). However, in the late 1980s, with the advent of the strong pound, increasingly demanding rules and regulations from Brussels, quotas, and, finally, the BSE outbreak, coupled with seriously falling returns, farming ceased to be such an attractive proposition and smaller farms became less viable; for example, though there used to be a number of dairy farms in the Parish, there are now only two, Overwood and Bank Top. So, as some farmers retired, some died and some landlords sold off their rented farms, these were bought by neighbouring farmers, or the sitting tenants, who would not have to find as much capital as any newcomer because they would already have had their buildings and machinery in place. This trend often resulted in the sale of the "extra" farmhouse and redundant farm buildings.

For instance, in Neen Savage on the West side of the River Rea, the farms at Stepple Hall, Stonehouse and Broome Park are now amalgamated while on the East side, part of Wall Town, The Nash, Cleobury Lodge, Lower Baveney and part of Upper Elcott are all farmed as one unit. From these examples alone, 4 of the original farmhouses are no longer occupied by farming families and the barns have become available and, once planning permission has been granted, converted into dwellings. In addition, cottages have been sold and many have been converted from the "2 Up, 2 Down" type to quite big houses - more into the "desirable residence" category. This puts them way beyond the pocket of those wanting starter homes or retiring pensioners wishing to stay in the area in which they have spent much of their lives.

However, this year it has been announced that land in Kinlet has been bought by the Shropshire Housing Association and, after some hard work by both the Association and Neen Savage Parish Council, eight new houses (4 X 2 Beds for 4 people and 4 X 3 Beds for 5) are to be built there and, because Neen Savage is part of Kinlet Ward, applications to become tenants, from anyone living in this Parish, will be considered. This vital addition to the local housing stock is, in no small way, thanks to the unflagging determination of the District Councillor, Mrs. Madge Shineton.

The Medical Centre in Pinkham, Cleobury Mortimer, still takes care of the general health of the Parish but with considerably more staff. There are now 3 Doctors and one G.P. Trainee, 1 Health Visitor, 3 District Nurses, working with 2 Auxiliary Nurses, 2 Practice Nurses and a Practice Manager with 2 full time and 4 part time Receptionists, of whom one works as a Secretary in the mornings and a Receptionist in the afternoons and another is a trained Phlebotomist, (taking blood on Monday, Tuesday and Thursday); in addition, there are 2 Midwives, one from Ludlow in attendance every Monday and one from Kidderminster every Thursday. A Chiropodist is available once a week and a Physiotherapist twice a week. However, great concern has been expressed, in the last few years, over the decision of the Worcestershire Health Authority to downgrade Kidderminster General Hospital with the removal of all services, including Accident and Emergency, except for minor injuries. The plan is to have just a few beds there for recuperation or day care purposes for walk-in, walk-out day patients; it seems that difficult or more complicated problems will, in future, be treated by "Telemedicine", whereby diagnosis and the necessary treatment will be given to the resident doctor via a T.V. Screen manned by expert consultants who may be many miles away! A new hospital is being built in Worcester, scheduled to be opened in 2002, and the Alexandra Hospital in Redditch is being up-graded but, overall, there will be less beds available than heretofore. There has been much objection to the plan and many public meetings have been organised to inform the "Powers That Be" of the overwhelming feeling of being "let down" which is engendered in this closure - but so far all to no avail. The many thousands of people in North Worcestershire, and South Shropshire, including those in Neen Savage, who have relied on Kidderminster General Hospital, will, in future, have to face travelling considerable distances for any long-term medical or surgical treatment (as will their visitors). In cases of Emergency, it might well come down to the discretion of the Ambulance driver as to whether the patient ends up in

Redditch, Worcester, Princess Royal Hospital, Telford or even the Royal Shrewsbury Hospital all of which are about 1 hour away from here! - Not a very satisfactory state of affairs. The fight goes on to have more services retained at Kidderminster General Hospital, at the very least an Accident and Emergency Unit, but the fear is that the present "Listening Government" just does not hear! Even as this is being written, coaches are taking 500 people to London, to take a petition to Downing Street and to see the Health Minister, Mr. Alan Milburn, though it seems he cannot find the time to meet them!!

Services for this Parish continue much the same as they have been since the mid 1950s when water, electricity and telephones were put in; in the 1980s the Parish was taken off the Elan valley water (Birmingham needed it all!) and put on to the water supply from Trimpley Reservoir and it must be said that the water from there, coming out of the River Severn, as it does, has to be fairly heavily chlorinated etc., so it is far from being as palatable as the Welsh water, though people are assured it is just as potable. There is no gas laid on but both gas and oil, currently the most favoured for central heating boilers or cookers, can be brought and stored in outside tanks. The Rubbish is still collected every Monday, (unless it is a Bank Holiday, when Tuesday is the collection day), and the bags still have to be put out at the end of the drives; one improvement is that a skip, in which larger household waste can be disposed of, comes to Six Ashes for 3 hours every other month.

The Postmen for Neen Savage are: Les Hunter, Brenda Chinn, Daphne Truck, and Kevin Draper, with Mike Worrall as Relief Driver; they deliver the post every morning, seeming, somehow, to get through whatever the weather throws at them. Because this is such a rural area, when they deliver letters, they will also collect letters for posting, and, given the money, will stamp the letters at the Post Office or bring stamps out with the next delivery; the service they give is excellent and very much appreciated by the Parishioners.

Only one bus for Bridgnorth now comes through the Parish, leaving Barbrook at 9.15 a.m. every Saturday and getting back at 12.40 p.m. However, another bus does go through Farlow and Oreton for Bridgnorth and there is a complete daily bus service to and from Ludlow and Kidderminster, which stops for passengers in Cleobury Mortimer; so, provided one can get into Cleobury Mortimer, transport is available. A bus for the school children in the Parish attending Lacon Childe School comes from Ludlow, and picks up the pupils in Oreton and Farlow, Stottesdon, and then past Shunesley to Six Ashes, reaching the School in time for the 8.45 a.m. start, and doing the route in reverse when taking the pupils home. Oreton and Farlow as well as Stottesdon have their own Primary Schools but the children in Neen Savage, going to the Cleobury Mortimer Primary School, board the same buses as the Lacon Childe pupils; some children from the Parish go to Kinlet Primary School and some attend the Primary School in Farlow for which a bus is provided, as the road was deemed too dangerous for walking. Other buses take Students to the VIth Form Colleges in Ludlow, Kidderminster, Bridgnorth or Worcester.

NOW, in July, 2000, it has just been announced that, under the auspices of the Bridgnorth District Rural Transport Partnership Scheme, (BDRPT), an Action Plan, which was launched on May 8th, includes a proposal to allow the existing Cleobury Mortimer to Bridgnorth bus service to operate twice a day, six days a week, allowing half a day in Bridgnorth; the service would be demand-responsive, i.e it would deviate from its core route if a passenger booked the service in advance, so the bus would divert from the main road, on demand, to any of the Parishes like Oldbury, Middleton Scriven, Deuxhill, Billingsley, Kinlet, Chorley, Sidbury, Stottesdon, Oreton, Farlow, or Neen Savage. Initially, the project, administered by the Countryside Agency, is to run for three years and is funded by Bridgnorth District Council, Shropshire County Council and the Countryside Agency along with the Community Council of Shropshire. The aims of BDRTP are to improve rural dwellers' access to shops, banks, libraries, health centres, employment, leisure centres, cinemas etc., to improve information about transport services, to integrate existing transport resources and to address social exclusion by reducing "unmet" transport needs. Basically, this would seem an ideal project in an effort both to help rural non-drivers and to reduce the number of people who feel they must use their cars, but much work on the coordinating of pick-up times and places as well as the disseminating of the necessary information has still to be done and it remains to be seen how it will all work out.

Shopping for most day to day items* can be done in Cleobury Mortimer which has a Chemist, a Bank, a Post Office behind a shop selling toys, stationery and fancy goods, two Butchers, numerous grocery stores, 2 bakeries, 2 ironmongers, a health food shop and a newsagent, amongst others; (David Jones who ran his newsagent shop for over 30 years has just retired, so William's shop across the High Street is now the newspaper shop). "Extra Special" sells clothes but only from size 16 upwards, so, for buying clothes, or anything like furniture and bigger household goods, shoppers go to Ludlow, Bridgnorth, Kidderminster, or even Birmingham, which towns, of course, also have their own supermarkets.

Brown's, from Cleobury Mortimer, no longer deliver bread in the Parish but

*For cost of items on a shopping List see Appendix III

it is still delivered, on Wednesdays and Saturdays, by Robert Link from Oreton, who has other groceries in his van as well; Lambert's Shop, from Tenbury, also delivers bread and groceries, stopping at Barbrook on a Friday. Mawley Town Dairy Farm, which lies just over the Neen Savage Parish border, produces milk and cream which are delivered to 45 houses in the Parish by Pain's Delivery Service and, just last year, Mawley Town Farm also started to produce some superb ice cream. Across the Parish on the north west border, Detton Hall Farm is producing Detton Beef and Lamb - fresh meat and/or freezer packs, ready to freeze or already frozen, which can be bought at Little Detton.

A Voluntary Car Service is run by Rev. Bill Elliot from Cleobury Mortimer, and Jane Smith, Jim Martin and Jenny Vanderhook are volunteer Drivers from the Parish; they take people to the Doctor, or for essential shopping, Hospital Visiting, (though not to hospital for treatment - the hospital, they are told, has its own car Service for that!), to the Old People's Club or to collect and deliver prescriptions. The voluntary Meals on Wheels Service is run by Mrs Gill Chapman, of Cleobury Mortimer, and presently Mrs. Pat Bryan is the only Driver, and there are no recipients, in Neen Savage. A Meteorological Observer Station for the MET Office was located at Nethercott and looked after by the late Gordon Lennox and Stroma, his wife, for many years, but when she left, to live in Cleobury Mortimer in 1994, the Station was moved to Detton Hall where it is now manned by Eric Ratcliff, with his son Arthur as a back-up.

The three biggest changes in the Parish in the last twenty years have been the advent of the Golf Club, the taking over of the City of Coventry School area by the Pioneer Centre and the building of the first Parish Hall in the Parish. Now that the Golf Club has a licence to sell drinks, it can no longer be truly said that there is no pub in the Parish and, with meals provided in their restaurant, there is now an excellent venue in which to exercise, eat and socialise. It is proving a first class amenity for Neen Savage.

The Pioneer Centre has brought further employment to the area, and people from all over the world are coming there to help in the work with young people, from the socially excluded, young offenders and youth at risk. The aim is to offer, through Sport, Creative Activities, Adventure and Training, opportunities which will assist all kinds of young people to achieve their full potential, - physically, emotionally and spiritually - while providing a caring, accepting and safe environment. For some of those who are visiting the area, it is a life-style changing experience, - an opportunity to realise a completely different environment with new physical and emotional challenges which jointly question accepted values and standards. This Parish provides these young people, both staff and visitors, with the necessary ambience in which to unwind and learn new values, in the peace and tranquillity of the lovely countryside all around their adventurous, creative Centre.

The Parish Hall has indeed proved as beneficial to Neen Savage as it was hoped it would be. The 7 Members of the Parish Hall Management Committee*, chaired by Clare Ratcliff, administer bookings and the day to day running and maintenance of the Hall with great success; a caretaker was employed to look after the bookings and cleanliness when the Hall was first opened, but this proved a bit expensive and not all that necessary so the Committee now do it themselves. The Hall was redecorated last year and pictures, some bought and some donated, have been hung on the walls, making the Hall look more homely. In the coming year, the Committee hope to build on a small extension, to provide better facilities for the disabled and further storage space. Constantly in use throughout the year for private parties, it is also a place where meetings can be held, where fundraising events can occur, be it for the Church, the W.I., the Hall itself or whatever, where concerts can be held, or even where Parishioners can just come together for "fun" occasions, and get to know each other better. All of this helps engender more of that Community spirit which seemed so sadly lacking in the late 50s, the 60s and 70s but which now appears to be returning, thanks to this Parish Hall. It is also the venue for a polling stantion, and for public meetings and enquiries. The organisations that have greatly benefited are the Parish Council, The W.I., and the Edwards & Hinckesman Foundation who can all now use this facility for their regular meetings.

The Parish Council*, with 6 Councillors under the Chairmanship of Eric Ratcliff, and the Clerk to the Parish Council, now meet every other month, with site- and other meetings when necessary. Much has been achieved in recent years, with regard to improving some areas and amenities in the Parish. A parking area with a picnic site has been made at Six Ashes; considerable tidying up, along with a long-term Management Scheme, under advice and assistance from Chris Butterworth, and with much help from the residents of Baveney Wood, has been carried out in the Baveney Common area, which belongs to the Parish Council, and there has also been a tidy-up at Pike Common. In addition, Notice Boards have been put up at strategic points around the Parish to keep Parishioners informed about what is going on.

The Women's Institute*, with their President, Mrs. Pat Bryan, have certainly benefited from having a regular meeting place. There are presently 25 paid up Members, which include the 9 Members of Committee, and Meetings are held

*For names of Parish Council and other Parish Organisation Members - see Appendix. 11

on the second Wednesday of every month, with the A.G.M. now taking place in November and the Produce/Handicraft Meetings in May. Sometimes Outings are organised instead of Meetings, like the visit to Daniel's Mill, near Bridgnorth, on August 9th, this year. The Annual Dinner is usually taken in July and this year is on July 12th at the "Live and Let Live" in Neen Sollars. It is, perhaps, interesting to note that of the 25 Members, 15 now come from outside of the Parish with 13 from Cleobury Mortimer, one from Highley and one from Kinlet; fifty years ago the majority of Members would have been the wives of either farmers or farmworkers in the Parish, but now there are no wives of farmworkers and only five farmer's wives, who are Members.

The Edwards & Hinckesman Foundation* is composed of 5 Trustees with Eric Ratcliff as Chairman. With the Vicar of the Parish, who is now the Revd. Preb. Robert Horsfield, Vicar in Charge of Cleobury Mortimer and the surrounding Parishes, there are two Trustees appointed by the County Council and two by the Parish Council. The Trustees meet twice a year. It is their responsibility to award funds from the Trust to help children of the Parish, usually from Secondary Modern or Comprehensive Schools, up to the age of 25 years, in any and every aspect of their education, including music, art, sport and travel. The income of the Trust has been reduced in recent years because of the fall in Interest Rates; in order to optimise the funds for grants, the Trust has dispensed with the professional services of a solicitor and accountant and are fortunate to have obtained the voluntary services of the Parish Council Clerk as Clerk to the Trustees.

The Parochial Church Council*, of 12 Members with the Revd. Preb. Robert Horsfield in the Chair, generally meet every other month at Baveney House, by kind permission of Church Warden, John Haywood. Recently they are having to meet more often because the Church is undergoing some costly repairs which, even with a grant from English Heritage, mean that the Parish has to raise some £27,000, requiring many different fund raising events to be organised by the P.C.C., in addition to the twice yearly Wine and Cheese evenings already held at Baveney House. It is hoped that the repairs, to the Tower, Roof and Guttering, will be completed some time in August and it is planned to have the two bells hung and ready to ring on the day of Neen Savage Celebration 2000. Neen Savage no longer has its own Vicar but does have a Curate, shared with Kinlet; unfortunately, after a mere two years or so, just as the Parishioners are getting to know him, and vice versa, the Curate leaves for a bigger Parish and the learning process has to begin all over again.

Last year, with the Millennium in mind, the Millennium Committee* was formed with 9 Members, under the Chairmanship of Clare Ratcliff. They are planning a grand "Neen Savage Celebration 2000", on September 16th, which includes a Photograph of all those who are there, a Punch and Judy Show, Sheep Racing, a Skittles Tournament and Treasure Hunt, all accompanied by the Bell Inn Brass Band along with a Pig Roast and Bar to be followed by a Fireworks display; there will also be a Flower Festival in the Church. A "Time Capsule" is to be placed in the Church containing a record of Neen Savage in the year 2000 and an Ecumenical Service is to be held later in the year when the Commemorative Spoons, to the children in the Parish - all 62 of them! - will be given out. At the same time a Millennium Oak, kindly donated by Brenda and Don Weaver, is to be planted. Meanwhile, Parishioners are taking snaps for inclusion in a Photographic Record of the Year in the Parish and, later in the year, there is to be a Wine and Cheese Evening, with a Local History Display, when this Book will be launched. In addition, new gates to the car park have been made and will be hung as soon as the repairs to the Church have been completed. To help with the funding of all this, a grant, from "Grants for All" under the "Millennium Experience" Fund, was received towards the cost of publishing this book, for some display boards for the Parish Hall and for the Photographic Albums; contributions also came from organisations and a very successful Promises Auction held earlier in the year raised quite a sum, with the proceeds being divided between the Millennium Committee and the Church. Meanwhile fundraising goes on.

The Editorial Board Members* of the Parish newsletter, "The Vital Link", meet every other month, at Detton Hall, to collate the news of what has happened or is going to happen in the Parish and Elisabeth Ratcliff, or Sue Del Mar when Lis is away, decides the format then types it out before taking it to Stuart Harding of S.J.H. Print, who prints it into 172 issues which the Editors deliver to almost every house in the Parish, and many in Cleobury Mortimer. Funded by the £1.50 yearly subscriptions, the advertisements and with a grant from the Parish Council, this newsletter has proved its worth over the years, keeping Parishioners informed and helping to advertise events in the Parish.

Neen Savage is very much a rural area but it is by no means a backwater. Modem Technology, which has swept over the country, has also been flowing into the Parish. Word Processors came first to a few homes and these were quickly followed by a few Computers and then Fax machines. Now, however, there are more computers, some of which are already on the Internet, and e-mail and mobile phones are on the increase. Nevertheless, it is a rural area and agriculture still pervades the scene. Whereas fifty years ago the production of food was the predominant aim, the emphasis has now changed to conservation and to this end many more trees have been planted and a number of farms and gardens have areas put aside for wild life, wild flowers, butterflies and birds, and "diversification" is very much in the minds of some of the farmers.

Meanwhile the River Rea continues to flow through our Parish creating, as it goes, so many beautiful and peaceful areas in this lovely part of South Shropshire. It is worth noting here that the Cleobury Mortimer Footpath Association have inaugurated the "Simon Evans Way" as a Millennium celebration of the South Shropshire Countryside. Simon Evans, looking for a job in the country air after being gassed in the First World War, became a postman working from Cleobury Mortimer and subsequently a writer and Broadcaster; his "round" went from Cleobury Mortimer up the Rea valley to Stottesdon and back. The Footpath Association have marked out a pathway of approximately 18 miles in the form of a figure 8, with Detton Hall at the crossover, which, though not following specifically in his footsteps, covers much of the way that Simon would have followed and grown so to love that he found he just had to write and talk about it all, in his books and on the Radio.

Though the population numbers of those living in the Parish have remained roughly the same, the occupations followed by the inhabitants not only vary considerably of themselves, but are all noticeably different to what they would have been at the beginning of the last century, and for many years before that; this is fully revealed in the following pages. The houses are all listed in alphabetical order and place names beginning with the word "The" are under "T", unlike the custom in telephone directories. Unfortunately, the news that The Lodge, (which was No 2. Wyre Farm), home to Amanda Salt and Steven Barlow, is now to be called "Harvest Edge" arrived too late as that part of the book had already gone to print, so it is still listed under "The Lodge".

Anmerlea

Anmerlea is a wooden bungalow built by the Birmingham Water Works to house workers on the pipe lines which were laid down to take the water from Wales to Birmingham. The bungalow can be reached by going down Ron Hill and then taking the right hand turn off the Green Lane; it is situated by the River Rea, near the viaduct that carries the 4 large water pipes across the river; the first pipe was taken across before the turn of the 19th century and the last one was laid in the mid-1950s.

At one time, Anmerlea was owned, as a housekeeper's cottage, by a Mr. Hughes who had three children: ANita, MERvin and LEA - hence the name of the bungalow! At the end of 1981, Anita Chance, who was a Higginson and married to Hugh Chance, moved here, having previously been at Hill House Farm, Milson; she has two daughters, Emma, aged 28, and Lucy, 16, who goes to Lacon Childe School. The bungalow has 3 bedrooms, bathroom, sitting room and a kitchen and there is a field in front of the house in which horses are kept.

Anita's Mother, Eileen Higginson, and her Aunt, Nancy, still live in Cleobury Mortimer along with other relatives.

April Cottage

April Cottage, formerly known as Jeff's Cottage, lies on the left hand side of the Kinlet - Cleobury Mortimer road, just inside the border between Kinlet and Neen Savage. Originally it was quite a small stone built cottage but it now consists of a utility room, kitchen, lounge and a downstairs bathroom with 3 bedrooms; this spring a 25 ft. 2 storey extension is to be added to make a lounge and a 4th bedroom, allowing the current lounge to become a dining room.

In April 1996, Nicholas John Spragg, born in Kidderminster, and his wife, Sheryl Ann (nee Lea-Hair) bought the Cottage and moved here from Kidderminster. They have two children: Jordan James, aged 5 and Fraser James, who is 3 years old. Nick Spragg owns a Roofing Company with his brother with whom he also does building and renovation work; he and his wife own 6 flats in Castle Road, Kidderminster and 12 Flats in Sutton Road.

Sheryl writes:- *The cottage was originally known as Jeff's Cottage. However people kept ringing up asking to speak to "Jeff" and, as my husband is named Nick, he was not very pleased! We decided to change the name to April Cottage as this coincided with the month we purchased the property. My parents used to live in Halesowen and we had a caravan at Riverside Caravan Park in Bewdley which we used at week-ends. It was during one week-end that I met Nick at Plato's Night Club at the Stourport Moat House. My parents then decided to move this way and we went to live in Highley for 9 years. My parents moved again, about four months ago, to Woodgates Green, Knighton-on-Teme while Nick's parents have lived in Kidderminster all of their married lives, though his Father was born in Shrawley, Worcestershire.*

Avelana

Avelana is a brick built bungalow which was put up in 1992, by J.S.R. Farms, to be used as a house for the Manager of the 300 Sow Breeding Farm on what used to be called Upper Baveney Farm. With an Agricultural Tie on it, it is composed of 3 bedrooms, bathroom, kitchen/dining room, living room, and a utility room and garage.

Geoffrey Massey and his wife, Maggie (nee Watts) were living here with their children but have now moved into Larks Rise in Cleobury Mortimer. In April/May, 2000, Simon Moore, who was born in Birmingham, came, from Madley in Herefordshire, with his wife, Maggie, (nee Brown), born in Walsall, as Pigman for Upper Baveney. They were married in Litchfield in 1992 and have two children - Robert, aged 6, nearly 7, who goes to Cleobury Mortimer Primary School, and Jessica, who is 3 years old.

The name Avelana comes from the Latin name for Hazel and was suggested by Maggie Massey's brother, Philip, in recognition of the Hazel hedge which surrounded the bungalow. Simon says that, as a keen gardener, he is looking forward to working in the garden.

Bank Top Farm with Musbatch

Bank Top Farm, situated on the bank above the River Rea, across from the Church, was a farm of 60 acres, but, farmed in conjunction with Musbatch, 35 acres, and 3 fields on the Church side of the river, bought from Lower Neen Farm when that was sold, and with other fields "off", it now totals 150 acres. It grows corn, rears sheep for lambs, and, carrying 48 Cows with followers, is one of only two dairy farms now left in the Parish*. A grain silo was built in 1997.

The house was built of brick in 1910 on the site of an old cottage and comprises 4 large bedrooms, with an attic, a sitting room, dining room, kitchen, back kitchen, pantry, bathroom and cellar.

In 1965, Raymond Herbert Pearce, with his wife, Annie Margaret (nee Dunn) took over from the Northwood's. They were married at St. Marys Church, Cleobury Mortimer in 1963 and have 3 grown up children: - Andrew Herbert, aged 35 (see Musbatch) - Dorothy Anne, 33, who married Steven McBride in 1990 and they live in East Kilbride and have 2 children, Kathryn Ann, aged 5 and Craig, aged 3, and - Jennifer Linda, aged 27, who works with Greenall Insurance, in Ludlow.

*The only other dairy farm now in the Parish is Overwood Farm.

Musbatch

Musbatch is a cottage-style black and white farmhouse dating back to the 16th Century; timber framed of brickwork and stone, it has a tiled roof. An old cowshed, which joined on to the house, was converted into a downstairs bedroom and a bathroom, and a large store room and a staircase were also installed. It now consists of a kitchen, utility room, breakfast room, dining room, sitting room, bathroom and 3 bedrooms.

Andrew Pearce, who was born in Ludlow, came to live here after he had married Alison, (nee Meston), born in Rushwick, Worcs, at St. Lawrence's Church in Wichenford in 1992; she was a Personal Assistant working in Shrewsbury and they have one daughter, Georgina, aged 3¾ years, who goes to the Little Learners Nursery School. The farm lies to the south of Bank Top and the garden, which faces south, has a small brook at the bottom. Both Bank Top and Musbatch are bounded on the east side by the River Rea and they have about ¾ of a mile of the fishing rights, that below Musbatch, and that from the Church to the water pipelines on the far bank; the fishing rights from the Ford down to Musbatch were retained by Mr. Geoffrey Schoelles.

Barbrook

This row of 10 semi-detached houses, lying on the left of the Stottesdon to Cleobury Mortimer road, just below the Baveney - Neen Savage cross-roads, was built in 1948 as Council Houses for local farmworkers, but this no longer pertains, and the present occupants follow diverse pursuits.

No. 1. Derek Pead, who was born in Tenbury, is a lorry driver who came to live here, in the 1960's. with his wife, Queenie (nee Millichamp), born at Angel Bank, Ludlow. They have 4 married children: Peter, who has two girls, Quinton, with one son, and Pippa and Susan.

No.2. Mrs. Annie Dorothy Viggars, (nee Leighton), widow of Daniel Herbert Viggars, who died in 1986, is the oldest resident in Barbrook having moved here, from Lower Baveney with her husband, in 1949 when it was first built. Her childhood was spent at Musbatch. She has one daughter Joy, who was married to Geoffrey Spearing but, tragically, he was killed in a car accident when their daughter, Elizabeth, was 12 months old. Joy, who is a teacher at a Primary School, has since married Ron Pearson and they have a daughter, Zoe, who is taking her G.S.E.s this summer. Elizabeth (nee Spearing) married Michael Worrall; their daughter, Lucy Anne was born 1.4.00.

No. 3. Consisting of 3 bedrooms, a sitting room, dining room, kitchen, 2 toilets and a bathroom, No.3 was occupied in 1982 by Suzan Elizabeth Gittens and her partner, Anthony Skellern, moving from Clee Hill; she now lives here with her younger daughter Marie, who goes to school, her son Michael, who is a factory worker and her elder daughter, Elizabeth, and her three children.

No. 4. Connie and Jack Philpotts came here in 1967. They have four children, all grown up and living away though Kevin, their youngest, still lives in Cleobury Mortimer from where he runs a taxi service.

No. 5. In 1960, Mrs. Violet Edith Howe (nee Greenwood), who was born in Chorley, came to live here with her husband Sidney, who, sadly, died in 1968. They have three children: Christine, Shirley and Robin. Mrs. Greenwood, mother of Mrs. Howe, came to live with her in 1969 and remained here until her death in the 1990's.

No. 6. Peter Joseph Price, who was born in Ludlow and is a warehouseman, came to live here 15 years ago with his wife Barbara Ann, born in Camborne, who is a cashier. They have three children who are all living in Cleobury Mortimer: - Roger, who is working with an Environment Agency, is married and has two children, - Wendy Skellern, married with one child, and - Lynda who is a Health Care Support Worker.

No. 7. This house consists of 3 bedrooms, a bathroom, 2 sitting rooms and a kitchen. Brothers Wilfred and Robert Pike have been here since about 1977.

No. 8. Mr. and Mrs. Pullings left here earlier this year, to go and live in Stourport. At the end of March, David Cound, who was born in Bromsgrove, and his partner, Tracy Whinnery, born in Birmingham, bought No.8 and are now busy redecorating and having the house rewired; it consists of 3 bedrooms, a sitting room, dining room, galley kitchen and an outhouse. David, who is a Unit Manager of a regional Secure Unit, has 3 grown-up children: - Alex who does Bar Work, - Danielle, who is hoping to go to University this September and - Christianne who works with computers and is getting married in August. Tracy is a Forensic Psychiactric Nurse and has 2 sons: - Shaun Anthony Cooper, aged 14 and - Rickie Lee Cooper, who is 8 years old and they both go to school in Solihull.

No. 9. Mrs. Annie Hinton, (nee Poyner), widow of Mr. John Hinton, who died in 1976, moved here from Oreton in 1959. There are four grown-up children: Brian, Michael, Trevor and Margaret. The house consists of 3 bedrooms, 2 sitting rooms, and a kitchen and recently a new bathroom has been installed with a new kitchen and new windows.

No.10. Mr. Reuben Evans, a mechanic by trade, who was born in Shrewsbury, has lived here since 1966, with his wife, Anne, (nee Perks), and their now grown-up children.

Baveney Acre, Baveney Wood

In 1987, David Roy Trevor, in the Automotive Industry, who was born in Birmingham in 1948, and his partner, Julie Ozols, a Personal Assistant, born in Kinver, bought Baveney Acre and moved here from Mamble. Julie writes that they are both keen on Country Pursuits, hunting, fly fishing, shooting and supporting the local point-to-point. Her Mother and Father were married at Kinlet Church almost 50 years ago and her father worked for the Smith's at Siligrove Farm before eventually settling in Kinver. Ray's parents were of Brosely origin and were farmers before moving to Birmingham where his father joined the Police Force and, eventually, opened the first D.I.Y shop.

The house is 30 years old, brick built and consists of a kitchen, dining room, living room, hall, laundry, 4 bedrooms, 2 bathrooms and a snooker room. It lies up the bank on the left of the Cleobury to Bridgnorth road, just after Wall Town Bridge.

Baveney Bungalow

Baveney Bungalow is made of brick and was built some 28 years ago as a staff cottage for Lower Baveney Farm; it consists of a kitchen, sitting room, hall, 3 bedrooms and a bathroom. It is currently unoccupied and stands on the right of Baveney Lane travelling from the cross roads by Old School Hall to the Kinlet road.

Bay Tree Farm, Baveney Wood

In 1995, Michael John Hurley, who was born in Birmingham, and his wife, Jacqueline Anne (nee King), born in Blackburn, moved here from Sussex. Married in Solihull in 1974, Michael is in Training and his wife is a Teacher;

they have two grown up daughters: - Angela, aged 24, is at University in Manchester and - Nichola, 21, is at the Further Education College in Derby.

Bay Tree Farm lies down to the right off the Baveney Common Lane entering it from the Kinlet to Stottesdon road; built of brick and stone, it has 5 bedrooms, a bathroom, 3 reception rooms, and a breakfast/kitchen room. All the windows have been replaced and general improvements carried out.

In the garden, the flower beds are being developed and trees planted.

Belle Vue

Belle Vue is a brick-made bungalow, built in 1952, standing on a corner of land near where the five roads meet at the cross roads known as Six Ashes.* It consists of 3 Bedrooms, 2 reception rooms, kitchen, bathroom, hall, toilet and 2 porches; new windows have been installed recently.

Mr. Anthony Walter Burke, a retired Comprehensive School teacher on Technical Subjects, and his wife, Olive May (nee Bracey), a Primary School and Music teacher, also now retired, bought the bungalow in 1953, moving from Burrow Cottage to live here in 1956. Both born in Birmingham, they were married there in 1947 and have two sons: - Michael Anthony, a Motor Vehicle and Agricultural Workshop proprietor, whose workshop is adjacent to Belle Vue; he lives in Bayton and was married to Lucy (nee Keig Shevlin) with whom he had two children, Richard and Jennifer, but is now married to Pippa (nee Beckett) and they have one son, Max. - Paul John lives in Borth and is a fisherman and general repair worker.

Mrs. Burke is a member of a Poetry Society and writes beautiful poetry.

*Six Ashes is where five roads from Bridgnorth, Kidderminster, Cleobury Mortimer, Neen Savage and Stottesdon all meet. Planted many years ago, six Ash trees gave this cross roads its name, but, one after another, they died or had to be felled and the last original Ash was cut down as being unsafe, in 1979. However, to commemorate Coronation year, the Parish Council planted 14 Ash Trees and 2 Rowans here in 1953 and 2 further Ashes more recently.

Beneliza, Overwood

This brick bungalow was built on a plot of land at Overwood Farm, in 1991-2, after John Griffiths, owner, had proved to Bridgnorth District Council that there was an Agricultural Need for a second dwelling at Overwood; planning permission was granted but only with an Agricultural Occupancy

Clause on it which means that only someone, who works in Agriculture or has retired from agricultural work, can live in any dwelling built on this plot of land. It was built so that John's son Kevin, could carry on living in Overwood Farmhouse. The bungalow has a sitting room, kitchen, laundry, lobby, 2 bedrooms, a bathroom, an office, conservatory and a garage.

John Benjamin Griffiths, who was born in Chelmarsh in 1936, and his wife, Joan Elizabeth (nee Milman) born at Clows Top in 1941, were married in Bayton Church in March, 1962 and moved in here, when it was finished, from Overwood Farmhouse. They have four grown up children: - Jennifer Mary married to William Worrall, living in Maple Close, Ludlow with their children, Kelly, Zoe and James. - John Charles, a Cocoa Trader, Cadburys, married to Rachel (nee Mellard), living in Sandpiper Close, Spennels, Kidderminster, with Thomas and Katie. - Kevin, married to Lucy (nee Birch) at Overwood Farm and - Sarah, married to Brian Bower, who lives at Bridgwalton Farm, Morville, Bridgnorth, with their son and daughter, Edward and Amy. John's brother lives at Overcott.

The name of the bungalow is taken from the first part of the second names of John and Joan!

Bowens Cottage, Baveney Wood

Formerly known as Bowens Place, Bowens Cottage was built, of local stone with a tiled roof, in approximately 1750. It has 4 bedrooms, a bathroom, 2 reception rooms, study, kitchen and 2 utility rooms with a ground floor W.C.

It is situated up on the left of the Cleobury Mortimer to Kinlet road, just beyond April Cottage which is on the right.

It was bought, in January, 1990, by Mr. Stephen Hinton and his wife, Gillian, who were both born in Birmingham and moved here from Wolverhampton. Mr. Hinton is a Chartered Surveyor and Mrs. Hinton, a Property Developer. There have been continuing renovations inside the house since 1984 and, in the grounds, the old dairy/stable block has been converted to provide self-contained accommodation; two additional patios have been made in the tiered gardens, along with a new wall and all-weather "menage". An additional $1^1/_2$ acres were purchased to make this into a Registered Smallholding of 18 acres and there has been an extensive planting of trees, with rare and unusual fruit trees, and clearing done, with the provision of pools and wetland areas for wildlife.

Broome Park Cottage

Broome Park Cottage is built of stone and is the last house on the right, after Little Stepple and before the Stonehouse; the ceilings, which were very low, were raised in 1934 at the same time as a bathroom was installed. It now consists of 2 bedrooms, the bathroom, a sitting room, and a kitchen.

In September, 1980, at Hopton Wafers Church, Derek Stanley Jordan, who was born at Crumpsbrook, married Dawn Martin, born in Ludlow, and they came to live in Broome Park Cottage. Derek is an HGV Owner/Driver, and at one time ran a transport business which is now scaled down and used for other enterprises; Dawn works in Stock Control. They have 3 children:- Neil, 18 years old is an Exhibition Contractor. - Lee, 15 and - Ellen Rose, 12, both go to Lacon Childe School in Cleobury Mortimer.

Broome Park Farm

Broome Park Farm is on the left side of the Catherton Road going to Cleobury Mortimer just inside the Parish Boundary; it is an arable and livestock farm of 86 acres.

Mr and Mrs Thomas, with their sons, began farming here in 1938. Mrs Thomas died in 1994, aged 91, but Ivor and Gordon carried on until 1999 when the farm was bought by John Evans, who was born in Wolverhampton in 1954, the son of Dick Evans of Curdale Farm in Cleobury Mortimer. In 1986, John married Catherine (nee Hartley), born in Sherrifhales, at St Mary's Church, Cleobury Mortimer. Catherine is an engineer and they have a boy and girl, Rebecca and Richard, who are both going to the Primary School.

The house and buildings, part stone, part brick and part half-timbered, are thought to be 350 years old. There are 6 bedrooms, 2 kitchens, 3 reception rooms, a bathroom and pantry in the house and various other outbuildings and the Evans' are undertaking "ongoing restoration". Sue Evans of Greenways is John's sister.

Burrow Cottage

Daphne Marjorie Pearson (nee Embrey) who was born in Nesscliffe, came to live here with her husband Frank, on the very day they got married at St John's Methodist Church in Shrewsbury on the last day of 1973. Their son, Christian, is a driver. Mrs. Pearson was a third generation butcher in Nesscliffe.

The Cottage, built in the late 16th Century of black and white half-timbering and stone, is thought to have the only thatched roof in the Parish. A sitting room was put on the east end in what, at one time, must have been the cow shed, as oak beams have been taken out both upstairs and downstairs to accommodate doorways; there are 2 bedrooms, with a landing attic upstairs, and a sitting room, bathroom, pantry, porch and the living room-kitchen, which has been done in the last 10 years, downstairs.

Bury Cottage

Bury Cottage is a small stone cottage, situated about a quarter of a mile down a rough road on the left, leading off the Hall Orchard to Cleobury Mortimer road; in 1995, it was completely renovated with an additional bedroom window added and in 1998 a conservatory was put on, so that now it consists of a bathroom, 2 bedrooms, kitchen, sitting room, and conservatory/playroom.

Andrew Ivor Price, who was born in Kinlet, and is a grandson of Mrs. Violet Price, the previous owner, and his wife, Jill Mary (nee Cope), born in Cosford, moved here after their wedding in Neen Savage in January 1990. Andrew is an Agricultural Contractor and Jill a Medical Secretary and they have three children: - Benjamin, aged 9 and - William, 7, who both attend Cleobury Mortimer Primary School, and -Sophie, who is 4 years old and goes to Peter Rabbit Nursery School. Andrew is the son of Evelyn Price of Woodend Farm and brother to Richard at The Old Barn. Jill is the daughter of John Cope, who is the Butcher, of many years standing, in Cleobury Mortimer.

Cherry Cottage, Overwood

Cherry Cottage was, up until about 1986, arguably one of the oldest untouched buildings in the Parish, 2 up and 2 down, still no bathroom, no flush toilet and all its water pumped! Built of half-timbering with no real foundations, it was said to be of the 11th Century and is situated down a rough lane to the left of the road from Hall Orchard to the Nash.

In 1990, Martin John Orgee, who was born in Worcester, and is a Managing Director, bought Cherry Cottage and came here from Cambridgeshire with his wife, Lucy Caroline, (nee Hambridge), born in Luton, who is a Company

Director/Secretary. They have two children living here: - Alexandra, aged 7, and - Jennifer, 6, who both go to Abberley Hall School, and – an eldest daughter, Sarah, living in Penrith, with their 3 grandchildren.

They refurbished the house, converting the cowstalls into rooms and extending the lounge in 1991 and making further alterations to the kitchen and a bedroom in 1998. Presently, it consists of 4 bedrooms, lounge, hall, dining room, kitchen, utility room, toilet and 2 bathrooms. They have also put up some stables and out buildings.

Martin and Lucy Orgee run their Valves and Controls Distribution Company from Cherry Cottage.

Chilton

Chilton is situated roughly in the middle of the Parish and is approached down a 1/4 mile long dog-leg drive flanked by mature Corsican pine trees. The date of the original house is not certain, but the earliest brickwork is typical of the period around 1690. However, this may be predated by the stone part of the house. The front half of the present house was added in the late Georgian period, around 1790, with typical features including a curved staircase, fanlights and carved architraves. At the end of the 19th Century, a second story was added to the Georgian part of the house, with dormer windows and a large wooden front porch.

In 1966, the front of the house was restored to its original Georgian appearance, with a parapet wall, reduced top windows and removal of dormers and bargeboards. The Victorian porch was replaced by a portico including Sicilian marble Doric columns rescued from a Staffordshire house and restored to their original condition. Since 1995, the house, which consists of nine bedrooms, 4 reception rooms and a kitchen, has been re-roofed and re-wired as well as redecorated and a tennis court and ponds have been installed in the garden; it has a front terrace and, behind the house, are the original coach house and stables.

In September 1995, Peter Michael Clarke, a Dental Surgeon with his practice in Bewdley, came here with his wife Suzanne Jane, (nee Biddle), after having lived for three years in Heightington House. He was born in Dudley, she in Stourbridge and they met while students at Birmingham University where Peter got his Honours Degree in Dental Surgery and Suzanne obtained her Honours Degree in International Studies. They were married in Churchill,

Blakedown in 1984 and have four sons, aged thirteen to seven: - Alexander who is at Cheltenham College, – twins, Edward and Joseph, and - Charles, who all attend Winterfold House School.

Church of St. Mary

An Extract from Kelly's Directory of 1895, as accurate 105 years later as it was then, says of Neen Savage Church: "The church of St. Mary standing on the east bank of the Rea is an ancient building of stone in the Norman and Early English styles, consisting of chancel, nave, south porch and an embattled western tower containing 2 bells. The spire which was of wood was destroyed by lightning in 1825 and has not been replaced. The east windows are stained and there is a beautifully carved oak screen between the nave and chancel. The church was restored in 1882 under the direction of Mr. Thomas Gordon, architect of London, at a cost of £1,300 raised by subscription, and an organ was erected in 1885. There are sittings for 175 persons. The register dates from the year 1575".

However, wear and tear have inevitably taken their toll and, in this year 2000, the Church is undergoing urgent repairs, under the direction of John Wheatley, the architect from Tenbury, to stabilise the tower with special ties, replace some of the stones and repoint the whole tower, with further work to be done on the roof and on the rainwater goods, including laying some new drains, all of which, this time, is going to cost around £123,000. Because St Mary's is a Grade II* Listed building, a generous grant of £96,000 has been given by English Heritage which leaves £27,000 to be found by the those in Neen Savage Parish, though other grants may be forthcoming.

Neen Savage is in the rural Deanery of Burford, which has been amalgamated with the rural Deanery of Ludlow. The Reverend Robert Horsfield is the Vicar in charge of the six Churches: Cleobury Mortimer, Hopton Wafers, Milson, Neen Sollars, Kinlet and Neen Savage. John Andrew Clarkson Sewell (Andy) was a policemam for 20 years, before becoming ordained a Deacon in Chichester in 1977; he was an Assistant Curate at Horsham when he was appointed Curate for Neen Savage on August 15th, 1999.

Andy, who lives at The Glebe House in Cleobury Mortimer, is married with three children: - Andrea, who is 16, - Thomas, 14 years old, and they both go to Lacon Childe School, and - Rosina, who was born in October, 1999.

The Church can be found opposite The Old Vicarage.

Cleanlyseat Farm

Cleanlyseat (pronounced "Klanleyseat"), which was, at one time, two words, is a brick and stone built house, on the edge of the Parish Boundary, at the end of a long drive, on the left, at the bottom of Ron Hill in Cleobury Mortimer. Parts of it are thought to be at least 200 years old, but it has been altered and added to over the years and, recently, an adjacent barn was replaced by a two storey extension; it now consists of a kitchen, 4 reception rooms and 3 bedrooms.

In 1993, David Eve and his wife, Gabrielle, (nee Wilson), who was born in Birmingham, bought Cleanlyseat and moved here from Rowley Regis; he is an Anglican Clergyman and Gabrielle is a teacher and they have one daughter, Susan, who is a Social Worker, living with her husband, Pete Owen, and son, Wesley, in Hamilton, Toronto, Canada.

The farm extends to 27 acres on which they raise sheep.

Clee View, Baveney Wood

Clee View is the first building on the left going up Baveney Lane from the Cleobury Mortimer to Kinlet road. It is a stone built house which has been virtually rebuilt. and has 12 acres of land with it. The house is owned by Yvonne Rogers and she has two sons: Thomas, who is at University and Edwin who is an Apprentice Farrier.

Cleobury Mortimer Golf Club

We are grateful to Graham Pain who wrote the following for inclusion in this book:-
Robert and Graham Pain were farming some 400 acres (160 ha) in a traditional system of Dairy Cows, Cereals and Sheep; part of this farming partnership occupied 150 acres (60ha) at Lower House farm. During the late 1980s to early 1990s, the brothers became increasingly concerned about the future prospects for the traditional small to medium sized family farm. Milk quotas had recently been introduced, that restricted expansion of the dairy herd, and other commodities were under pressure from increasingly low world prices, coupled with less political will to support rural industries.

After much research and study, it was decided to move the business emphasis away from agriculture to a land based leisure industry. Having done further market research in conjunction with the English Golf Union, it became apparent that there was a substantial market for Golf so long as it was of good quality and priced competitively.

Seeing this as a challenge, the brothers did further research and, in January 1992, plans were submitted to the Bridgnorth District Council for a nine hole Golf Course and a small Clubhouse on 70 acres (29 ha) of land at Lower House Farm. The design of the Course had an emphasis on maintaining as much as possible of the natural beauty of the area and enhancing it with the planting of native trees and shrubs. Planning Permission was granted and, with local Contractor Phil Price commissioned to do all the earth moving, work was started in June 1992.

The Club opened on July 1st, 1993 with 202 Members and quickly gained a reputation for quality Golf in a friendly atmosphere. Within a year, plans were put forward to extend the Course to 18 holes and to enlarge the Clubhouse. By July 1995, the Course had become 18 holes and the Clubhouse had 2 bars, a snooker room and extended locker rooms and, most importantly, the Club had 500 Members and a growing list of regular visitors.

At this time, the Club covered the entire land formerly known as Lower House Farm. In the Spring of 1997, an opportunity arose to acquire a further 45 acres (18ha) of land adjacent to the Golf Course from the Robinson family of Mawley Town Farm. A decision was made to extend the Course by a further 9 holes, giving three loops of nine holes and relieving a lot of the pressure that was building up at peak times due to the popularity of the Club which, by now, had 700+ Members.

In this Millennium Year, Cleobury Mortimer Golf Club boasts a 7,000 sq. ft. Clubhouse, car parking facilities for 120 cars, a modern greenkeepers facility, 27 holes and 3 practice areas covering 200 acres (81 ha). It now has 760 Members, 15 full time staff and 5 part-time, and is the only Licensed Premises in the Parish of Neen Savage.

Cleobury Lodge

Cleobury Lodge is at the end of a long drive off to the right, just beyond Wall Town House, on the Cleobury Mortimer to Bridgnorth road. A three storey farmhouse, it was built of brick and stone in the 18th Century and consists of 6 bedrooms, bathrooms, 3 reception rooms and a kitchen and has recently been augmented with a utility room and a conservatory type addition to the kitchen.

John Morland Del Mar, who was born in Chalfont St. Giles, bought Cleobury Lodge in 1976 and moved here with his wife, Susan Caroline, (nee Capel-Cure), born in Moreton-in-Marsh, from Winchester. John, who is in Industrial Management and Sue, a retired teacher, were married in Aldershot in 1964 and they have two grown-up children: – Hugo John, married to Francesca and living in London, and - Anna, who is married to William Hellier with two children and they are living in Australia for just one year.

Cleobury Lodge Barn

The original stone-built barn, on Cleobury Lodge Farm, is thought to have been of the 17th Century; it was converted to a house, with planning permission as a Holiday Let, in 1992; it consists of 4 bedrooms, a bathroom, 3 sitting rooms, kitchen and back kitchen.

George Edmund Haywood, born in 1969, son of John and Christine Haywood, of Lower Baveney, married Emma Lucy (nee Darlington), born at Nantwich in 1966, at Marbury in Cheshire and they took up residence here in 1996. They have twin sons, John Edmund and Guy William, aged 2^1/$_2$ years, and a daughter, Sarah Georgina, 9 months.

The Lodge Farm of about 176 acres is part of the Lower Baveney Farming Unit; diversification includes fishing and Christmas trees sold wholesale.

Clump Cottage

Clump Cottage lies on the right, about 100 yards down from the Old School Hall cross roads, towards Nethercott. Somewhat hidden behind bushes and trees, this is a very old stone built cottage which consists of one bedroom upstairs, a small hall and sitting room downstairs with a kitchen extension built on at some time.

Mrs. Alice Stretton bought Clump Cottage in 1961 and it is now owned by Mr. Walter Stretton.

Detton Barn

Detton Barn, lying down by the River Rea, on the left of the road to Oreton, below the line of the old railway, is the last of the buildings to undergo conversion to a dwelling, which was done here in the mid 1990s. It was bought in August, 1999, by Ivor John Caswell, a Civil Engineer Director, and his wife, Valerie Lesley, (nee Groutage), who were both born in Birmingham. They are still living in Tamworth while in the process of rectifying some of the conversion work in the house, which was so poorly carried out previously; they hope to move in, around June 2000, as soon as the bulk of the work, of which they are doing the majority themselves, is completed. The house consists of 3 bedrooms, bathroom, lounge, kitchen and dining room.

Ivor and Valerie Caswell have three grown up children: Neil Ivor, a Civil Engineer Director, married to Gillian (nee Marshall) from Newcastle, living in Tamworth. - Darren Peter, an Architect, who is married to Mary (nee Stann), born in the U.S.A, and living in Michigan, and - Emma, who is a Laboratory Assistant and lives at home.

Detton Cottage

Detton Cottage is a small stone cottage in the middle of the field, on Detton Hall Farm, which was known, for many years, as Chapel Meadow. The meadow was the site, in 1960, of an archaeological dig looking for signs of the Mediaeval Village; a few shards were discovered and foundations noted, but most of the village had entirely disappeared and it was also proved that the cottage was NOT the old chapel as many had thought. The stone cottage was probably built in 1800 and consists of 3 bedrooms, a lounge, kitchen and bathroom, with a Porch added in 1994 and a garage in 1997.

Albert John Thomas, who was born in Wem, moved here from Albrighton in 1991, with his wife, Carol Ann (nee Parkinson), to work on Detton Hall Farm. They have three sons: - Stuart Dale, aged 10, and – Bejamin David, aged 7, who both go to Farlow School, and Harry Adam, aged 16 months.

Detton Hall

Detton Hall, easily recognised by its tall Tudor chimneys, lies at the northern end of the Parish and is the second farm down the road from Hall Orchard to Oreton. Probably a manor house, no longer here, stood where the walled garden is now, but its half-timbered crosswing still stands as the west wing of the present house; continuing eastward is the central section, still half-timbered on the north side but now stone clad on the south. There is yet another part to the east that is stone built. Using dendrochronology, a purlin in the

South View

crosswing roof has been dated as "felled in spring of 1573", thus that part of the house was probably built in about 1575. There is also a positive dating of 1729 for the roof of the central section, but there is ample evidence that this is a second roof, the original one (early 17th century) was of stone tiles.

Starting in 1991, under the supervision of English Heritage, extensive restoration work was undertaken, aided by a grant towards major repairs on the chimneys, roofs and timber framework. In the process, shingles, corrugated iron, pebble dash and cement render were removed from various outside walls and upwards of 1500 cu. ft. of home grown and sawn oak were used to replace extensive areas of the timbering where decay and beetle damage had taken their toll. Twelve blocked windows were revealed; a stone built annexe, replacing a corrugated iron shed, was added to provide a toilet, workshop and wood store, and the cellars reinstated; work is still in progress on the West Wall half-timbering, the granary and steps at the East end, and on the outbuildings, consisting of a Hackney stable, traphouse and the pig sties.

Detton Hall* now consists of two staircases, a large kitchen, a pantry/dairy, a patio room, living room, study/office, a hallway, dining room and drawing room on the ground floor, 4 bedrooms and 2 bathrooms with the granary room on the first floor and an attic bedroom, with a small windowless room leading off it, on the top floor, reached, from the kitchen, up a spiral staircase which has a one piece 22 ft. newell post. At a slightly higher level, there is a large attic, originally windowless but now with two dormers, used as a playroom, with a quaint "belvedere" at one end; at the west end of the house, at the top of the Elizabethen staircase, which has cut-out panels instead of balusters, there are another two attic rooms. Some of the rooms are oak-pannelled. There are also two cellars, under the crosswing, still as original but with improved drainage.

In agreement with English Heritage, visits, to see the restoration work, can be arranged by prior appointment

In 1952, Eric Charles Ratcliff, who was born in London, and his wife, Elisabeth Brodie, (nee Gurney-Dixon), born in Brockenhurst, Hampshire, came here as tenants to Major Woodward, of Hopton Court, but they bought the house and farm from him in 1977. They were married in Winchester Cathedral in 1945 and had 5 children: - Julia Maureen married to Mike Thomas in 1976 and they farm at Stoke Manor, Stoke-on-Tern with their son Nicholas Charles, in his Final year studying Archeology at Camarthen University, and daughter, Amanda Louise, doing her A-levels this year and hoping to go to Lancaster to read French with English as a Foreign Language this September; unfortunately Mike has recently suffered a stroke so they are moving later this year to Strefford. - Piers Gurney, who lives near Denham, Suffolk. - Samuel Charles, who was killed in a road accident, aged 19 years, and is buried in Neen Savage Churchyard. - Arthur John, who married Clare Elizabeth (nee Taylor) in 1980, and, in partnership with his wife and parents, now farms Detton Hall Farm. (See under Little Detton) - Kim Louise Brodie married Paul Hinwood, of Withypool Farm, in 1983, and they farm there with their 3 children; Erica Joanna, who will be 14 in August, and Jessica Louise, 12 years old, who both go to Lacon Childe School, and Jack, 8, who is at Hopton Wafers Primary School.

Considerable work has been done in developing the garden and a small grass paddock, planted with trees and bushes, has been added, with a ha-ha built to the south, replacing a hedge and ditch, to give a wider view down the valley.

Detton Mill

This building was an old flour mill and used as such until about 1930, when the big water wheel collapsed and the then Landlord, Admiral Woodward, was unwilling to get it repaired and, in any case, not so many farmers were bringing their corn to be ground. Subsequently it became somewhat derelict. However, in the middle of the 1980s, the Mill was converted into a residence with many of the original features being retained. On three floors, the upper two floors comprised the main living areas and included 3 double bed rooms, a family bathroom, a living room, dining room and kitchen. On the ground floor, an additional shower room/toilet and a large utility room were created. In 1999, the utility room was fully renovated into a working kitchen, with the addition of a new window overlooking the weir, and the kitchen upstairs was gutted to create a fourth bedroom-cum-additional living room.

On December 11th 1993, in Queen's College Chapel, Cambridge, Bryan Stiles, who was born in Coventry in 1959, was married to Alison Everest, (who decided not to take the name of her husband but to retain her maiden name), born in Bromsgrove in 1963, and they bought Detton Mill in February, 1996, as their U.K. homebase. Although currently living and working overseas, they spend 6 weeks a year back over here, so that they can be close to their families in Shropshire and Coventry, and they intend Detton Mill to be their family home for many years to come.

They are both bankers - Bryan has been on the International Staff of HSBC for 15 years and Alison was on their International Staff for 10 years before finishing work to look after the twin boys, Thomas Edmund Rhys and Matthew William Owen, who were born in Hong Kong on August 1st, 1997.

Detton Mill House

Detton Mill House used to be just Detton Mill, but, in the late 1970s, the Mill was sold for conversion to a home, and later the barn was also converted, so now there are Detton Mill House, Detton Mill and Detton Barn all situated at the bottom of Detton Bank, between the River Rea and the old Ditton Priors - Cleobury Mortimer Light Railway line, now disused, though its path can still be easily traced.

In the early 1980s, Mr. Ron Jones bought the house from Mr. Christopher Woodward and, with his wife Belinda, set about the tremendous task of restoring this 450 years old timber-framed stone house to its former beauty, (without changing the looks too much), and installing a bathroom and inside toilet! They also converted the pigsty into a garage and stables.

Since then it has changed hands once or twice, and a lobby, conservatory and bedroom above the kitchen have been added. Now it consists of a lobby, kitchen, living room, dining room, entrance hall and conservatory downstairs with 2 bathrooms and 4 bedrooms upstairs.

In April, 1998, Peter George Hallet, born in Barnstaple, and his wife, Jan (nee Williams) born in Swansea, bought the place and moved here from Rye in East Sussex. Married in Swansea in 1962, Peter, who was a Computer Software Engineer and Jan, a Cattery Proprietor, are both now retired.

Dinmoor

Sometime in the last two centuries DinmoOR became DinmoRE, but, in old 17th century maps, it is clearly marked DinMOOR, so the present owners have decided to keep to that name. It is situated on the right side of the Cleobury Mortimer to Bridgnorth road near to the "Wet Reins" Coppice and was originally two cottages; of ship's timbers, stone and home-made bricks on a sandstone base, with a stone-tiled roof, it is thought to have been built sometime in the 16th Century. It comprises 4 bedrooms, a bathroom, kitchen, living room, dining room, stairs and hallway with a utility room, a downstairs W.C. and a rear hallway.

In 1994, Paul David Flowers, born in Birmingham, and his wife, Angela, (nee Wood), born in Widnes, bought Dinmoor and moved here from Holly Cottage, Netherton, Highiey. They were married in St. John Fisher, Widnes in 1977, and are both teachers; Paul is teaching at Redhill, Stourbridge and Angela is at the Hagley R.C. High School. They have three children: - Jacob Jonathan, born in 1981, - Nathan Paul, aged 16, and - Naomi Clare, who was born in 1986. They have no near relatives in the Parish, though there are some relatives of Angela's Uncle.

Goesland

Goesland stands up a bank on the right of the road from Detton to Nethercott. Originally a small cottage built of stone in the late 1600s, it has had quite a lot of work done on it over the years by first, a Mr. Larner and then Mr. Arthur Butterworth, who bought it in 1956 and added a kitchen to the 2 rooms downstairs and 2 more bedrooms upstairs and a bathroom. His daughter, Roz, inherited Goesland after his death, and, with her partner Derek, knocked the four bedrooms back to two, so the house consists of a living room, kitchen, dining room, pantry and porch with 2 bedrooms and a bathroom. Tragically, Roz died on July 6th 1995 after a long fight with cancer and it then came to her brother Christopher.

Though Christopher George Arthur Butterworth, who was born in Kidderminster while living in Wolverly, lived here as a child, when his parents used it as a holiday cottage before moving here permanently in 1981, it was in 1996 that he moved back, coming from Aston Botterel with his wife, Tamara Katherine, (nee Staples), who was born in Coventry. Chrisopher is a Countryside Ranger and Tamara a Teacher and they have two children:- Annie Elizabeth, who is 14 and a gifted musician attending Lacon Childe School, and - Ellen Katherine, 13, who also goes to Lacon Childe School in Cleobury Mortimer.

Since coming here they have installed a shower and enclosed the garden with a wall. They are a Registered Smallholding of 7 acres of woodland, an orchard and pasture, with a vegetable and fruit plot, all managed as a Nature reserve.

Greenways

Greenways lies on the left at the top of Green Lane, before the junction with Catherton Road and is a brick bungalow, built about 1967. It consists of a kitchen dining room, sitting room, bathroom, 2 bedrooms and another sitting-cum-bedroom.

In 1982, Susan Margaret Evans, born in Wolverhampton, and a Farmer, moved here from her parents farm, Curdale, Cleobury Mortimer, and lives here with her partner, Jeffrey Lewis, born in Welshpool, who is a Service Engineer. Susan has a brother at Broome Park Farm, and she is a niece to Margaret Griffiths at the Pound House and cousin to John, at Lower Elcott.

Hillfields

Hillfields is the first house on the left of the road from Mawley Town to Six Ashes and was built in 1945 as a temporary accommodation for workers laying the water pipeline from Wales to Birmingham.

Originally timber framed with asbestos cladding, a brick skin was added in 1976, and the bungalow consists of 3 bedrooms, living room, kitchen, bathroom and W.C.

Roy Kennet, who was born in Tottenham, and his wife Alice (nee Collins), born in Blakesley Towcester, Northants, bought Hillfields in 1974, and moved here from Bridgnorth. Though both are now retired, Roy was a herdsman for 15 years and then became a Foreman Wood Machinist and Alice was a Kitchen Assistant; they were married at Fawsley, Northants in 1950 and have six children: - Andrew Guy, a warehouse man, married to Carol (nee Finney) and living in Rugby has 2 daughters and a grand daughter. Rosemary Clare does part time office work while reading Local and Regional History at Exeter University, lives in Ivybridge, Devon, and is married to William Greene, with one daughter and a grandson. - Keith John, who is serving in the R.A.F., married Linda and they have 2 sons and 1 grandson and live in Stamford, Lincs. - Judith Rosamond married Martin Reaper and they are farming near Daventry, Northants with 2 sons and one daughter. Judith is a twin to - Ian Douglas, a self employed builder, married to Valerie (nee Wilde) and living in Market Drayton with one son and two daughters. - Alison Kay lives in Beeston, Nottingham and works in Boots Factory. All of which means that Roy and Alice Kennet have 11 grandchildren and 3 great grandchildren!

The Kennets maintain a lovely garden, open, sometimes, for the public in the summer and, comparatively recently, have installed a polytunnel in which they grow tomatoes and courgettes and many different and beautiful fuchsias.

Hillside

Hillside is a brick-built house, probably built around 1920, lying on the left of the Bridgnorth to Cleobury Mortimer road just before it meets with the road from Kidderminster. A two story house, it has a very steep pitched roof which gives it the appearance of a larger house. The loft space has been converted to an attic bedroom and another bathroom created, so it now consists of 5 bedrooms, 2 bathrooms, 3 reception rooms and a kitchen; there are also 2 garages.

David William Shackleton, an Electrical Engineer (retrd), who was born in Burnley, Lancs, moved here, from Stourport-on-Severn, with his wife Margaret (nee Mann) in 1982. They were married in Briercliff in August 1963. David is presently Organist for the Parish Church, Clerk to the Neen Savage Parish Council and the Edwards & Hinckesman Foundation and Margaret is a school teacher; they have two married sons: - Andrew William, an Insolvency Consultant, married to Suzanne (nee Phillips) and - John David, a teacher, who is married to Louise Amanda, (nee Coles), with one daughter, Helena Margaret Lynda, born January 5th, 2000; they all live in Bewdley.

Hillview

Hillview is another of the bungalows which were built by the Birmingham Water Works to house the workers laying down the water pipes from Wales to Birmingham and the inspection chambers for these underground pipes, which lie just outside the Bungalow, can still be seen.

Originally wooden, the bungalow was bricked round about 1989 and now consists of a living room, kitchen, 2 bedrooms and a bathroom.

Mr Albert George came to live here as a school boy 60 years ago; he is married to Brenda (nee Ainsworth) who came from Lancashire, and they have one son, Selwyn, who married Jacky Blood, from Bayton, in June 1983 and they live in Cleobury Mortimer.

There are 2 acres of land on which are kept a few sheep and some poultry.

Holly Cottage, Baveney Wood

Holly Cottage has a brick built front and stone built back and could be around 250 years old. It is sited down the Baveney Common Lane, on the right between the fork down to Bay Tree Farm, and Woodbine Cottage; it consists of a kitchen, lounge, dining room, cloakroom, study and utility room downstairs and 4 bedrooms and a bathroom upstairs.

Front

Stanley Thomas Kench, who was born in Stourport, moved here as Joint Owner with his wife, Ann Elizabeth, (nee Blencowe), born in Kidderminster, from 19 Somerleyton Avenue, Kidderminster, in July 1972. Stan retired in 1990 when he was Deputy Head of Northcote High School, Wolverhampton and Ann was a teacher at Lea House School, Kidderminster before retiring in 1988. They were married at St George's Church, Kidderminster, in 1960 and have 4 grown-up children: – Jacqueline Ann, a Tax Consultant, married to Nicholas Patten and living at Twigworth, near Gloucester. - Sarah Elizabeth, a Publishing Circulation Manager who was married in Kinlet in 1984 but is now divorced and living in Epsom. - Andrew Charles Thomas, a Rank Odeon Cinema Manager, married to Vilma, (nee Ramirez), living in Ickenham, Middlesex and - James Alfred Stanley, a teacher and Head of the Drama Department, who lives in Banbury.

Keeper's Cottage

Also known as Windy Harbour in days gone by, Keeper's Cottage can be reached at the end of a long track which leads off to the right on the road from the ford to Stonehouse. Originally a stone built one up, one down, with a small kitchen, it was sold off the Hopton Estates to a Mr. Coombes, who did a lot of renovation work on it and enlarged it so that it now consists of 2 bedrooms, lounge, kitchen and bathroom.

In 1995, it was bought by David Griffin, who was born in Blackheath, and his wife, Carol, (nee Brookes), born in Dudley; they were married in Kidderminster in 1990 and moved here from Stourport on Severn. They have six grown up children, of which four are David's by a previous marriage, and 4 grandchildren. Carol's Mother and two brothers live in Cleobury Mortimer and she has a sister in Clee Hill. David Griffin runs his own Paint-finishing Company.

Ladywood Cottage

Ladywood Cottage stands on the left of the Kinlet to Stottesdon road, just before the turning down Baveney Common Lane. Considerable renovations have been undertaken recently and it is currently the home of Mr. and Mrs. Peter Sisley.

Little Detton

Little Detton, brick-built in 1982, lies on the left of the road to Goesland, just below Detton Hall. Since it was built, it has had another bedroom and office added, and now consists of 4 bedrooms, a bathroom, kitchen, living/dining room, spare room, and office. Outside, there are a double garage and small unity for handling, packing and storing home produced meat and, behind the garage, three wooden horse stables.

As soon as the house was finished, in September 1983, Arthur John Ratcliff, a Farmer, son of Eric Ratcliff, of Detton Hall, moved in from Kinlet, with his wife, Clare, (nee Taylor), who was born in Pinner; they were married at Long Crendon in 1980 and have three children: - Tanya Marie, 15 years old, - Steven Gurney, aged 13, both attending Lacon Childe School, and - Suzanne Dawn, 10, who goes to Farlow Primary School until July.

The farm was owned co-jointly with Severn Lodge Farm, Kinlet, but that was sold in 1992 and later, two fields were brought from neighbouring Richard Whitehouse of Prescott Farm, so now, Arthur and Clare, in partnership with his parents, farm Detton Hall Farm, which currently extends to 160.3 hectares, (approximately 400 acres), producing beef cattle, sheep, beans and cereals. As a diversification "Detton Beef & Lamb" now sells home produced meat, fresh or frozen, in packs or simple joints. In addition, Clare has an all weather horse arena on the farm which she uses for schooling horses and teaching.

Little Overwood

Little Overwood lies at the end of a rough lane on the left of the road from Hall Orchard to the Nash. Built of stone-covered "wattle and daub" it bears the name of what was once a small hamlet in this area and probably dates from the late 1500s to early 1600s. It consisted of 2 connecting bedrooms upstarrs with a bathroom, hall, kitchen, and living room downstairs. An extension has now been built on to provide a lounge, another bedroom, and an upstairs bathroom; there is also a utility room and conservatory.

Brian Divall, who was born in Brighton, married Maggie (nee Alibut) born in Cheltenham, in Kidderminster in 1994 and they moved here from Bewdley when they bought Little Overwood in 1996. Brian is a Tax Manager and Maggie a Contracts Manager and they have three grown up children: - Stephen Bloore who is a Scenery Designer/Maker, living in York with his wife, Susie and their two children; - Christopher Bloore, a Sales Representative, married to Louise and living in Sussex; and - Damon Divall.

Little Stepple

Situated on the right of the road from Catherton towards Stonehouse, Little Stepple farmhouse is about 200 years old, built of brick and stone, and consists of 3 bedrooms, a bathroom, dining room, living room, hallway, kitchen and pantry.

In 1935, Mr. Edward Turner and his wife, Reada, bought the farm; Mr. Turner died and, in the autumn of 1999, Philip John Turner, her grandson, moved here from Oaklands to be with Mrs Turner, carrying on his Farming and Contracting Business; sadly, she died, aged 98, in October 1997.

The farm extends to 238 acres and is mainly arable and Cider Making, with an Animal Feed Business.

Little Stepple Cottage

Little Stepple Cottage is a brick built cottage that was erected about 1920 and has 3 bedrooms, a bathroom, dining room, lounge and kitchen.

Graham and Angela Morris came here in the 1970's but, sadly, Graham died in 1994. They had 2 children, Theresa and David; Angela and Theresa have now left but David, who was born in Ludlow in 1975, still lives here pursuing his occupation as a gamekeeper.

Little Wyre Cottage

Little Wyre Cottage, some of which is thought to date back to the 15th Century, is part of the "Campus" of the Pioneer Centre having previously been purchased by the Coventry Authority in 1964. It has a stone ground floor and a half-timbered first floor which has been rendered; the gable is brick built after it literally fell down in the 1960's. The cottage consists of a kitchen/dining room, a lounge, 3 bedrooms, a bathroom, utlility room and a large garage and store room.

On March 1st, 1999, Stephen John Robertshaw, who was born in Congleton, and his wife, Sarah Ann (nee Selden), born in Bury, moved here from the Furlongs Road in Cleobury Mortimer. Robert, who is the Operations and Fundraising Manager for the Centre and Sarah, a part time Forestry Commission Field Officer, were married in April 1989 at Hildenburgh in Kent and they have two children: - Richard Kevin, born in January, 1992, and - Alistair John, born in December 1993, who both attend Cleobury Mortimer Primary School.

A pitched roof has been added over the bay windows in the front of the house with double glazing put into the windows on the ground floor and into one in a front bedroom. A chicken house has been erected in the back garden, and areas added to provide for vegetables and fruit.

Stephen is the son of Ryland Robertshaw, Operations Director of the Pioneer Centre, who lives in Cleobury Mortimer.

Lodge Farm Bungalow

Lodge Farm Bungalow can be found up the lane, to Woodcock Cottage, off to the right of the drive to Cleobury Lodge. A wooden structure, with an asphalt roof it was put up some 70 odd years ago and consists of 2 bedrooms, sitting room, kitchen, bathroom and dining room.

In 1998, Gerald Edward Bryan, who was born in Neen Savage, moved here from Onibury, Craven Arms, with his wife, Naomi Beryl Ruth (nee Jones), born in Long Meadow's End, Hopesay Parish. Gerald, a retired Pearl Insurance Agent, and Beryl, a retired Teacher, were married in Neen Savage and they lived at Dinmore from 1962 until they went to Onibury in the 1980s; they have two grown up children: - David Edward Jones is a shopkeeper, running the "Salad Bowl" in Cleobury Mortimer, selling vegetables, fish, game and flowers etc., and married to Sharon Julie (nee Reeves) and they live with their two children, Emma Louise and Thomas Peter, in Lark's Rise, Cleobury Mortimer. - Sarah Emma Naomi, a Housewife, is married to Duncan Macintyre and they have two children, Jemma Naomi and Benjamin Peter and live in Craven Arms.

Gerald Bryan is brother-in-law to Pat Bryan at Stepple.

Lower Baveney Farm
(Baveney House)

Lower Baveney Farm, now called Baveney House, is one of four farms (i.e. the Nash, Upper Elcott, the Lodge and part of Wall Town) being farmed by the Haywood family, making a total of 700 acres in Neen Savage and 200 acres in Kinlet; they grow potatoes, as their main crop, mostly on contract for McCain Chips, plus sugar beet, wheat, barley, sheep and timber, and also provide fishing and shooting.

Baveney House was brick-built in 1964 for John Hayward, then at Wall Town, and his wife, Christine, (nee Woolrich), from Bridgnorth, to move into after their wedding in Bridgnorth in 1965. The house consists of a kitchen, dining room, sitting room, lounge, sun room, hall, and utlility room downstairs, with 4 bedrooms, and a recently enlarged bathroom upstairs, and a shower room.

John and Christine have two married children; - Sandra Estelle, 32, married to Andrew Bryan and living at Six Ashes, Bridgnorth, with their son and daughter, Ben and Ellen; and George Edmund, 30, married to Emma (nee Darlington), at Cleobury Lodge Barn, with their twins, John and Guy, and

South View

daughter, Sarah.

John's mother lives at Wall Town House, and his brother at Wall Town Farm; Frank Dorrell, of Neen House Farm, is a second cousin. John has been a Church Warden at St. Mary's Chruch, Neen Savage for 20 years.

Lower Elcott Farm

Lower Elcott Farm lies just about in the centre of the Parish, down the lane past Pound House; in the year designated as "The Year of The Tree" in the 1970s, the W.I. planted a white chestnut in the middle of the field behind Pound House, deeming that to be the exact centre of the Parish. The farmhouse, a Grade II listed building, is a 16th century house with only minor alterations to its original form. The farm is still farmed by the Griffiths family.

Lower House Farm, Wyre Common

Lower House Farm, lying at the end of the lane on the left leading to the Golf Club, between the Pioneer Centre and Mawley Town Farm, was originally built of brick and stone some 200 years ago, but it was completely rebuilt, renovated and extended in 1989 - 1999; in 1997 an extra bedroom was added and the lounge area enlarged, a garage was built on and a patio added to the rear garden. The house now consists of 4 bedrooms, a bathroom, kitchen, lounge, study, and shower room.

At Easter, in 1989, Graham Douglas Pain came here from Cleobury Mortimer, with his wife, Sara Louise (nee Straughton), born in Bamford, near Sheffield, a mid-wife working at Ronkswood, Worcester. They were married in Cleobury Mortimer in 1988 and have two children; - James Oliver, aged 6, who goes to Cleobury Mortimer Primary School and - Amelia Alice, aged 4, attending the Noah's Ark Nursery School in Cleobury Mortimer.

Graham is the owner of the Golf Club which he founded with his brother, Robert, and they have built a 7,000 sq. ft. Clubhouse, which, with ancilliary buildings and the 27 hole Golf Course which has been made, now covers 200 acres of former farming land. (See Cleobury Mortimer Golf Club).

Lower Ladywood

Lower Ladywood stands on the left coming down Baveney Common Lane from the Kinlet to Stottesdon road, some yards down from Ladywood Cottage. Living here are Janet Pepper and Paul Rogers.

Lower Neen

James Cecil (Jim) Hulme has lived here all his life, taking on the tenancy (to Mr. Roger Turner of Arley Estates) when his father John retired in 1970. In 1968, he married Gillian Helen, (nee Dickenson) from Bridgnorth and they have two daughters: - Jane Ann, and Vicki Louise, who now lives in Cleobury Mortimer with her two sons, Kyle James and Charlie Alexander.

The House, built in the 16th Century, or possibly earlier, was originally two small cottages, one of stone and one half timbered, divided at what is now the kitchen doorway and the dining room; it consists of 4 bedrooms, bathroom, shower room, 2 attic rooms, lounge, kitchen, dining room and pantry.

Jim bought the farm, which extended to 130 acres, as a sitting tenant, in January 1985 and sold 85 acres in April 1985. In 1994, he sold one barn and the buildings with 38 acres to Andrew Price, then one barn and 2 acres to Richard Price, keeping the old farmhouse with 4 acres of land.

Maywood Cottage, Baveney Wood

The original brick and stone part of Maywood Cottage is probably well over one hundred years old, but during the 1980s the then owners had various extensions built on so that it now has 4 bedrooms, a lounge, a sitting room, dining room, kitchen and bathroom. It stands on the left down Baveney Common Lane just below Holly Cottage, which is on the right.

In 1999, Colin Bannister, born in Birmingham, and his partner, Caroline Hillier, who was born in Bristol, bought Maywood Cottage from a Mr. and Mrs. Parsons, and came to live here, from Bromsgrove, in March this year. They are both Computer Systems Managers working for B.M.W.

Meadow Bank

Meadow Bank is a white-washed brick bungalow which was built in 1934 and stands on the left of the road shortly after crossing the ford on the way to Stonehouse crossroads.

It was bought in 1988 by Derek Jones, who was born in Llandrindod Wells, and his wife, Sara, (nee Field) born in Kidderminster, and they moved here from Stourport. They were married in Astley in 1982 and he is a Regional Manager for Sovereign Finance, while Sara teaches Music at the middle school in Stourport. They converted what had been the bathroom into a hall, one bedroom into an office, built an extension to include a bedroom, bathroom and utility room, and did a loft conversion to make a third bedroom, so now the bungalow consists of a kitchen, utility room, an office, lounge, dining room, hall, bathroom and 3 bedrooms.

Melbury

Melbury lies to the left of the road from Six Ashes to the Church, just before Neen House Farm which is on the right. The bungalow, named after Melbury Hill in Dorset where the previous owner spent happy times in her childhood, was brick-built about 1957, on $1^{1}/_{2}$ acres of former glebe land, and this was augmented by a small area, bought in the late 70s, which was part of the Cleobury to Ditton Priors railway line.

Philip Martyn Price, an Agricultural Contractor, who was born in Stourport, married Tracy Green, who was born in Southampton, at Neen Savage in 1986 and they bought Melbury and moved here from Bayton Common, Clows Top, in 1996. They have 3 children:- Robert John, born in 1989, - Martyn Philip, who will be 10 years old in September, and - Andrew David, who will be 8 years old this August; all three go to the Bayton Church of England School. Philip is now the owner of the old railway goods yard and has permission for 9 light industrial units to be erected on the site.

There has been quite a lot of work done to the bungalow which now consists of 4 bedrooms, which have been extended, 1 ensuite bathroom, an office, sitting room, dining room, utility room and a kitchen, also enlarged. Philip's Mother, Mrs Alma Price, his sister-in-law, Anne, his nephew and niece, Mark and Sarah, also live in the Parish. (See No 2 Railway Cottages).

Neen House Farm

Francis Leonard (Frank) Dorrell and his wife, Una, (nee Howells) came to live here in 1987 from the Day House, Stottesdon; Frank had bought the property from Mr F. P. Davies in 1966 but his parents, Thomas Leonard and Enid Dorrell, lived here until their deaths. Una was born at Ingardine, Farlow in 1926 and in 1950 married Frank, born in Wallfurlong, Stottesdon in 1922, and they have two daughters, - Helen Elizabeth who is a teacher and business partner now married to Richard Edwards with one son, Robert, living in Tenbury Wells, and - Eunice Ann, teacher and farming partner married to Michael Evans, farmer, with two sons, George and Charlie, and they live at the Day House in Stottesdon.

Neen House is built of stone at the front and brick at the back and consists of an entrance hall, lounge, dining room, sitting room, kitchen and larder downstairs and five bedrooms, two bathrooms, with a separate W.C. upstairs;

there is also a cellar and coal house.

There are 31 acres of land of which 13 are arable and the rest is pasture with the exception of two tree plantations - one being part of the old railway line which was purchased back to the farm. The main enterprise is sheep farming.

Nethercott Farm

Nethercott Farm house, which lies to the right on the lower road to Detton, is thought to be 16th Century and is half-timbered, with a stone frontage and extension added in the 18th Century, brick gables from the 19th Century and a later Victorian extension. It consists of 4 bedrooms, one kitchen, 2 reception rooms, office, cellar and 2 toilets; the east end of the house (separated in 1863) is in the process of being repaired and modernised to provide a further bathroom, bedroom and office.

Both Nethercott and Reaside Farms, along with others, were originally inherited from the father of, or bought by, the Carpet Manufacturer, Sir Geoffrey Tomkinson, who bequeathed Nethercott to his son, Nigel Tomkinson. He and his wife, Diana Joy, (nee Fisher), a piano Teacher, born in Barnes, London, took over the running of the farm in 1994, on the death of the then tenant, Gordon Lennox, and came here to live in 1995. They have three grown up children: - Christopher, (see Reaside), - Diana Heather, who, in 1984, married John Freeman, who runs a Plant Hire Firm, and they live in Brosely with their 2 daughters, Jessica, who goes to Shrewsbury High School and Annie, at Primary School. and - Michael.

Soon after they moved here from Heightington, sadly, Nigel died, leaving the farm to Michael. The farm, from down by the River Rea on the west, rising to 600 ft. on the east side, where the boundary is the Stottesdon road, extends to 250 acres, including what used to be Reaside farm; producing combineable crops and provision of grass keep, Michael is now concentrating on the production of coppicing products with coppicing, and the regeneration and restocking of new and existing wooded areas. The pond in the "old" orchard has been re-established and the "new" orchard restocked.

Nethercott Cottage

Nethercott Cottage, which was two farm cottages until 1963, when it became one, has some parts of it dating back to the early 16th Century, with the rear of the cottage having a wealth of beams and the front being of stone. The cottage consists of 3 bedrooms, 2 sitting rooms, a kitchen and bathroom.

In 1973, Reginald Thomas Wall, a Motor Mechanic, and his wife, Beryl Doris, (nee Nevey) moved here from Bagginswood; they were both born in Kidderminster and were married at Arley in 1953. They have 2 grown up daughters: - Susan Elizabeth Wheeler, a Civil Servant, married to Michael Bourne and living in Buckton, Leintwardine - and Melonie, who lives in Cleobury Mortimer.

Newbridge House

Newbridge House and Nursery stand on the left just before crossing the bridge over the River Rea on the Kidderminster to Cleobury Mortimer road. The house, which is about 170 years old, is built with a mixture of stone and brick and has 2 bedrooms, bathroom, sitting room, dining room and a kitchen.

The property of about 5 acres, which is classed as a small holding, is jointly owned by Marion Parsons, (nee Porter), who was born in Stourbridge, is a qualified teacher and came here, from Stourbridge, in 1977, and Michael Longmore, born in Kidderminster and a qualified Professional Engineer, who came in 1986 from Stourport on Severn. Michael has a son, James, who lives in Bewdley and is working for a Financial Services Company, and Marion's son, Bruce Phipps, is working in Information Technology and living in Evesham.

Newbridge Nursery was started in 1988 and, currently, Michael and Marion are running 2 other local small businesses: Newbridge Computer Services, and "Pets and Petals", a shop in Cleobury Mortimer selling flowers, plants and pet foods, and equipment.

Newhouse Farm, Baveney Wood

Built in about 1850 of brick and stone, Newhouse Farm has had a single story 25 ft. stone extension built on, facing south. It contains 3 bedrooms, a bathroom, 3 sitting rooms and a kitchen., and stands on the left coming down Baveney Common Lane, just after the fork to Woodbine Cottage.

In 1975 David Tedham, who was born in Croydon in 1939 and is a lecturer in Art and Design, married Hilary, a Potter and Sculptress, in Kidderminster; they bought Newhouse Farm and moved here from Rock, in August 1979. They have two children: - Tamsin, who is 16 and attends VIth Form College, and - Ashley, 15 this year, who goes to Lacon Childe School in Cleobury Mortimer.

Oaklands

To be found on the right of the Catherton road between the Stepple Lodge and Stonehouse, (which are both on the left), Oaklands is a seven room bungalow which was built in 1965. Mr. Roy Turner, whose son Philip Turner lives at Little Stepple, is the present owner/occupier.

Old School Hall

Still known as "Old School Hall", this was built in 1875 as a Church of England School for Neen Savage and stands almost in the middle of the Parish, on the crossroads between The Nash and Barbrook. The School closed in 1964 and was bought by Mr. and Mrs. John Bryan who sold it in 1967 to David and Joyce Mills. The building then underwent extensive alterations, was virtually gutted and turned into a bungalow consisting of 2 halls, 3 bedrooms, a lounge, dining room, kitchen, bathroom and separate toilet; two existing windows were lowered and a bay window put in on the north side with a portico built on to the west side.

In 1979, David Mills, who was born in Walsall and his wife, Joyce, (nee Howell), moved here from Birmingham, where Joyce was born. Mr. Mills runs his own business.

Old School House

In 1829, Richard Edwards bequeathed to his nephew and the Vicar, the Rev. Somer Cocks, the sum of £400 to invest in land and to pay for a schoolmaster to teach reading, writing and arithmetic to "20 poor boys of the Parish". It is stated that there was a small building which was used as a schoolroom until it seemed necessary and "desirable" that a school house and school room should be erected out of the funds of the John Hincksman charity and that the rent of 2/6 (12½p) a year should be paid by the Vicar and Churchwardens. It appears that the School continued as such until 1888 when it was closed and the buildings later turned into two separate cottages.

In 1963, Patricia Ann Treves (nee Thompson) came to see the Ford and discovered the cottages empty, and almost derelict, and subsequently they were purchased by her parents, Mr. Weston Thompson and his wife Jessie (nee Edwards) and knocked into one house. After Jessie died in 1998, the house was bequeathed to Pat, a retired Dental Surgeon, who was born in

Birmingham, and she now lives here with her husband, Barry William Treves, born in London, a retired Chartered Patent Agent and European Patent Attorney. They were married in Neen Savage in 1963 and have two grown up children: - Katherine Frances, born in 1966, a Doctor in Clinical Psychology, married to Dr. David Hadley and living in Venezuela with their 6 month old son, Thomas Simon; and - Richard Weston, born in 1969, an Hydrologist, who lives in Birmingham.

The house stands back up the bank on the left, just before reaching the Ford and currently both house and garden are in the process of conversion.

Although they do not have any relatives living in the Parish, Pat, on her Mother's side, can trace Edwards ancestors back to the 1700s, living variously in Bitterley, Caynham and Hopton Wafers.

Old Town Station Bungalow

Set back on the left of the Cleobury Mortimer to Bridgnorth road, by the old railway crossing, the Old Town Station Bungalow, which retained the name of Cleobury Town Station right up into the 1980s, was built of concrete by the Abdon Quarry Company about 1919. Originally housing the railway offices, (tickets etc.), it was converted into a dwelling in the early 1970s and now consists of 2 bedrooms, sitting room, bathroom, conservatory, and a kitchen which has recently been extended.

Hazel Eveline Draper, a telephonist/receptionist, who was born in Taunton and married in Far Forest, moved here 5 years ago from Bewdley. She has one son, Ian, who went to Bewdley High School and is now a Carpet Designer. Previously, Hazel worked at Mullers for 4 years and lived in Cleobury, where her Mother and married brother still live.

Overcott

Overcott, reached down a long drive, on the left after the turn to Overwood, is a two-bay oak framed cottage, with a stone chimney stack at the west end, and dates from the 17th Century. The stone front was added later. It contains a kitchen, bathroom, living room, sitting room, 2 bedrooms and a cellar. The kitchen was built on the end of the house approximately 100 years ago.

Overcott was purchased with Overwood in 1922 by John Mottershead for use by farm workers, but after his death in 1939, his widow Mary came here to live with their daughter, Mary, from 1940 until Mrs Mottershead died in 1979. In the early 1980s, Miss Mary Mottershead left Overcott and lived in one of the Papermill Cottages until her death.

In 1966, James Thomas (Jim) Griffiths, an Architect, grandson to Mrs. Mary Mottershead and brother to John Griffiths of Overwood, married, in Neen Savage Church, Joanna Evans, a Graphic Designer, born in Newport, Mon. and, coming in 1985, they presently occupy the cottage and are often visited by their grown up family of: - Lucy, an Architect, married to Gary Milliner and living in Bristol with their two sons, Finlay and Sam; and - Hannah, who is a Literary Agent living and working in London.

Overwood Farm

To be found down the first left hand side, unsealed road, between Hall Orchard and the cross roads, Overwood Farm of 171 acres, with 17 acres at Cleobury and 13 in Farlow, carries 50 cows and is now one of only two farms in this

Parish producing milk, whereas, back in the 1950s, milk producers in Neen Savage were numbered in the teens. The farm also has 60 beef fattening cattle, 160 ewes producing fat lambs and 60 acres of grain. Since 1984, 2 cattle sheds have been built - one, 75ft. x 35 ft. in 1986 and one, 45 ft. x 40 ft. in 1989, with a sheep shed, 24 ft. x 45ft.

Since his Father, John Griffiths, of Beneliza, retired in 1992, Kevin Frederick Griffiths, who was born here in 1968, has taken on the farm and lives here with his wife, Lucy Jane, (nee Birch), who was born in Doddington in 1976 and is now working with a firm of Solicitors in Stourport on Severn as a Legal Cleric, training to be a Legal Executive. They were married in September 1998 in Neen Savage Church.

The stone and brick built house is thought to be around 350 years old and consists of a back kitchen, kitchen, living room, sitting room, hall, toilet and 2 unused rooms downstairs, 6 bedrooms and a bathroom on the 1st floor with more presently unused rooms on the 2nd floor; there are open fire places in three downstairs rooms and two bedrooms; it also has a cellar.

Papermill Cottages

The Paper Mill, from which these brick-built cottages, erected some 150 years ago. derived their name, was burnt down about 1885. There were originally 8 cottages, but when Mr. Eric Tomkinson, of Rose Hill, inherited them from his Father, Sir Geoffrey, in 1946, he modernised them and knocked the two top ones into one and also the two at the bottom end. These cottages are numbered from the bottom of the hill upwards so, working from the top, there are:-

No. 8. In 1975, Patricia (nee Blount), a Housekeeper and Gardener, born in Bewdley, came here as tenant. She was joined by Robert Handley, a Builder, who was born in Hayley Green in 1940, when she married him in Tenbury Wells in 1977. They have 4 married children and 10 grandchildren:

- Susan, who married Bob Lawrence, and they have Christopher and Nicola, living in Bayton.
- Josephine, wife of Richard Atkinson, with Matthew and Rebecca, who live in Kidderminster.
- Marion, married to Steven Cox and living at Kingswinsford with Mark, Joanne and Kimberley.
- Patsy, married Robert Fletcher, and they live in Stourport and have Jennifer, Thomas and Alexa.

The cottage consists of 3 bedrooms, a sitting room, living room, kitchen and bathroom. A garage has been built on, and the garden has been dug out at the side of the house.

No.3, 4, 5, and 6 are unoccupied.

No.1. In 1992, Derrick James White, who was born in Cradley, and his wife, Jane Esther (nee Hill) born in Hayley Green, Hagley, moved here as tenants from Clee Hill. They were married at Old Hill in 1956 and have a daughter, Shirley Anne, married to a Flight Lieut. in the R.A.F, and living in Oxfordshire with their two children, Mathew, aged 12 and Rosie who is 9 years old. Mr. and Mrs. White are now both retired but he was an Optical Glazer and she was a shopworker.

The house consists of 3 bedrooms, a bathroom, sitting room, dining room and kitchen. In 1993, Mr. and Mrs. White created a small garden with a pond opposite the house and a photograph of part of this was included in the Cleobury Mortimer Millennium Calendar.

Parklands

Parklands was built of brick about 31 years ago when there was an agricultural restriction on it, but that has since lapsed. The house consists of 4 bedrooms, bathroom, study and a lounge/diner.

In 1999, James Howard Martin and his wife Marian Joy (nee Martin) bought Parklands from Don and Brenda Weaver, the original owners, who went to live in Cleobury Mortimer on Don's retirement. Jim, who was born in Kenton, Middlesex and was a Paper Mill Manager, and Marian, born in Sevenoaks, Kent, a Teacher in Drama and English, were married in 1959 in Rochester and are both now retired. They have three grown-up children: - Stephen James, a University Reader at Warwick, is married to Harriet and lives in Birmingham with their two children; - Philip Timothy, a University Lecturer at Greenwich, who is married to Wendy, lives with their three children in Sheerness; - Hazel Alison Sally, a Playwright and Director, married to Graham, has four children and is living in Clifton-on-Teme.

Since coming here, the Martins have extended the lawns and erected a summer house. Jim and Marian are the "Parish Link" for Age Concern.

Pioneer Centre

The original buildings on this site were in red cedar wood, brought over from Canada, and erected in 1939 by the National Camps Corporation, a subsidiary of the King George V Jubilee Trust, to be used by children from city areas to give them some experience of life in the country for short periods during their school years. However, when the Second World War broke out, the buildings were taken over by the Coventry Education Authority to house boys evacuated before the threatened air raids, which eventually took place. In 1957, the C.E.A. bought the premises to provide a boarding school for boys from Coventry and, in 1965, new buildings, for better science laboratories and more accommodation, were erected. In 1981 the decision was taken by Coventry City Council to close the School and develop other activities on the site which included Manpower Services and YTS training schemes. In 1987, the site, which was very run down at this time, was purchased by British Youth for Christ, (BYFC), as its National Headquarters, and they invested a large amount of time, money and enthusiasm into the centre, giving it a Canadian theme.

The Northamptonshire Association of Youth Clubs (NAYC) took on the ownership of the site in 1991 with BYFC continuing to have its National Headquarters based here until 1996, when they moved their headquarters to Halesowen, to be closer to the motorway links, though they continue to use the site and facilities for many residential events, as do other Youth organisations and family groups as well as charities and even industry, albeit the centre is alcohol free and the buildings "no smoking".

NAYC is an independent charity, which has been established for 36 years and was started by a Baptist Minister, Rev. Harry Whittaker, to establish Youth Clubs and support and co-ordinate their work in the county of Northants, but that soon spread to surrounding counties. The benefits of a residential experience were established 25 years ago and activities have been developed over the years so that the residential experience can be used to help develop the whole child mentally, physically and spiritually in a wholesome, caring, Christian environment. NYAC has set up its own trading company, to run its four centres, named Action Centres UK Ltd and their aim is to run the centres without making a loss; non-profit making, the fees the children pay cover only the cost of running the centres - maintenance and refurbishment are funded by the Charity which raises money by gift income from trusts, industry, individuals and even the occasional legacy.

PIONEER CENTRE. Showing Wyre Farm at top and the Cottage, Wyre Common – bottom right.

There are four centres of which the latest is Pioneer, covering 25 acres of land with 25 separate buildings and able to accommodate up to 145 people. This centre is staffed by a team of 20 full and part time staff, supported by up to 30 volunteers, from many different countries as well as the U.K., who join for one year at a time, live on site and receive pocket money.

Ryland Robertshaw is the Operations Director who lives in Cleobury Mortimer and he writes that they now have planning permission for a major building re-development of the site for which £1.5 million has to be raised; a group of supporters has been gathered together to seek sources prepared to fund such a project.

The Bungalow, 1 The Pioneer Centre

One of the original timber buildings, built 60 years ago, the bungalow consists of 2 bedrooms, a bathroom, dining room, living room and kitchen. Kristopher Jon Kirby, who was born in Burnley married Elaine Joyce Palmer in Leaholm, N. Yorks in July 1995 and they moved here from Ashton in Makerfield, near Wigan, two months later. They have one daughter, Sophie Rebekah, aged 7 months; Kristopher is an Outdoor Pursuits Instructor and Elaine is a Midwife, though currently a full time Mum.

2 Pioneer Centre

Also one of the original timber built bungalows with 2 bedrooms, lounge, dining room, kitchen and bathroom, No.2 has a garden. David Michael Moreton, born in Wolverhampton in August 1969, married Gayle Dawsson, born in Bury St. Edmunds in 1970, at Colchester Baptist Church in July 1991 and they moved here in April 1994; he is the Catering Manager and Gayle, the Office Administrator and they have one daughter, Charlotte Elizabeth, who was born on the 29th July, 1999. David's Mother, Mrs. C. Moreton lives in Cleobury Mortimer.

4 Pioneer Centre

Erected 35 years ago this building is steel framed - the Pioneer Centre Forest Lodge - and has a bed-sitting room, kitchen and bathroom. In September 1996, Donna Louise Marshall, a Trainee House Manager, moved here from Stoke-on-Trent, where she was born in 1977.

Pound House

Pound House, so-called because the village pound was situated at the top of the drive, lies on the right of the drive going down to Lower Elcott Farm, and is a brick-built house which was built by Mr. and Mrs. Bert Griffiths in 1980, when their son, John, took over the farming of Lower Elcott, and they moved up here in September of that year. The house consists of 3 bedrooms, 2 sitting rooms, kitchen and bathroom.

Margaret, (nee Evans), was born in Cleobury Mortimer and she has 3 grown up children: - Marion, a farmer's wife, married to Derek Lewis, and living with their children, Anne and Michael, in Berrington. – John, who is married with 4 children – Thomas, Ben, Joanna and Nicholas; and – Peter, who works for the National Trust and is living in Kent with his wife, Elizabeth.

Nos. 1 and 2 Railway Cottages

These two Railway Cottages, which are semi-detached, lie on the left of the main Cleobury Mortimer - Bridgnorth road, just before the old railway crossing. They were built around 1920 to house the employees of the Ditton Priors and Cleobury Mortimer Light Railway; constructed of concrete sections, they were made at Abdon works then transported and erected at their present site. After the closure of the railway line in 1963, they were sold off.

Mr. Alan William Stokes, an Electrician, who was born in Birmingham, bought No.1. after his marriage to Barbara in Rock Church in 1963, and they moved here from Blissgate. He is now divorced. There are two grown up children:- Adrian James, an ANC Delivery man, divorced and living in Cleobury Mortimer and his sister, Yvonne Louise, who is married and a Housewife also living in Cleobury Mortimer.. The house has been brick-skinned and consists of 3 bedrooms, a sitting room, kitchen and bathroom.

Mr. Robert Price and his wife, Alma, bought No 2. from a Mr. Davis, but after Bob's tragic death in a microlight accident in 1990, their eldest son, David, who was born at Bayton Common, came from Clows Top to join his Mother, with his wife, Anne, (nee Scarlett), whom he had married in Neen Savage Church in 1977, and they bought the Cottage in 1993. They had 2 chidren, now grown up:- Sarah, 21, who is in her Final Year at Birmingham, training to be a Teacher and - Mark, 20, a Mechanic working at Tim's Garage in Cleobury

Mortimer. Anne works in the A & E at Kidderminster Hospital and David was in Haulage but, sadly, he died from cancer in January 1995, and Anne has now put the house, which consists of 3 bedrooms, lounge, dining room, kitchen and bathroom, on the market.

Meanwhile, Mrs. Alma Price is living in the garden of No 2. in a fully equipped Mobile Home, which she is now hoping to be able to move to the grounds of Melbury where her second son, Philip, lives. She also has 2 daughters who are both now divorced, - Jennifer lives in Ludlow and works at Bitterley School, and - Tina, who is a remedial teacher at Bitterley School, living in Clows Top. Alma has 12 grandchildren and 3 great grandchildren.

Reaside Farm

Reaside Farm, of about 90 acres, is now being farmed in conjunction with Nethercott Farm by Michael Tomkinson. Part of the Tomkinson Estate, it was given by Sir Geoffrey Tomkinson to his daughter Mrs. Freeman, who rented it to Geoffrey and Elizabeth Bishop, but, when they moved to the Stone House in 1980, it remained empty for several years until Christopher Tomkinson, a banker and nephew to Mrs. Freeman, bought it and moved here from Knighton, Powys, in 1994. Christopher Hugh Tomkinson, who was born in London, married Jane Sarah Temple, born in Windsor, in Nether Alderly, Cheshire and they have three children: - Alicia, aged 12, - Katie, 9 years and – Isobel aged 5, who all go to Moor Park School, Ludlow.

Reaside house, down a long drive on the left of the road from Nethercott to Detton, is a 300 year old black and white half timbered building, with a later brick-built Georgian addition, and has 5 bedrooms, 2 sitting rooms, a dining room, kitchen and larder. Since coming to Reaside, Mr. and Mrs Tomkinson have renovated the farm buildings into guest bed and bath, a workshop and a playroom and, in 1997/98, they built a swimming pool and relandscaped the garden in 1999.

Christopher is the elder son of Mrs. Joy Tomkinson of Nethercott.

Rose Cottage, Baveney Wood

Rose Cottage and its workshop were built for the Lloyd-Baker Estate, in about 1815. The workshop was originally a Carpenter's shop and, in more recent times, has been used as a Blacksmith's. In 1875, the house was extended to provide a room for use as a shop to sell coal, sugar, butter etc. to the Estate workers. It stands on the right going up Baveney Common Lane, above the Old Forge.

From the time it was built to the present day, it has been occupied by the Lane family and their descendants and currently living there are the joint owners: Beatrice (nee Lane) Rogers, who worked at Mullers until her retirement, and her daughter Brenda Lewis, a clerical worker, both of whom were born at Rose Cottage. In 1963, in Neen Savage Church, Brenda married Ivor Lewis, a chainmaker, who was born in Stratford upon Avon and they have two grown-up sons: – Alan, married to Alison and living in Riding Mill, Northumberland, with two daughters, Catriona and Fiona, is in computing. – Stephen, an electronics engineer, is married to Anne and they live in Hawarden, Flintshire.

Rose Hill

Rose Hill can be found down the road that leads off to the right after the old railway crossing over the Bridgnorth to Cleobury Mortimer road. Built mainly of brick, the back part was constructed in about 1740 but the four front rooms were added by a Mr. Hall, the owner of the Paper Mill, in 1864.

In March 1947, the property came into the ownership of Eric Tomkinson and his wife, Margaret, (nee Steers). He died in 1979, but his widow still lives here.

School House

As its name implies, School House was brick built, for the Head Teacher, in 1875, at the same time as the Church of England School, to which it was attached. The School closed in 1964 and in 1967 it was sold off and the School House was detached. Originally it consisted of a hall, dining room, lounge, pantry and a very small kitchen which was enlarged soon after the house was purchased but then, in 1979, it was further enlarged by adding a new hall and dining room downstairs and two bedrooms and a toilet upstairs.

Anthony John Glaze, a Barrister, who was born in Bridgnorth, bought the house in 1996 and moved here, from Wolverhampton, in December of that year with his partner, Lesley Langley, who was born in Derby and was a teacher at Cleobury Mortimer Primary School. Sadly she died in March of this year. Since 1996 some exterior restoration work has been carried out and a conservatory built on.

Shunesley Farm

Shunesley, which is the first farm on the left, down the road from the Hall Orchard towards Detton, is made of brick and stone and dates from about 1680; it could be said, arguably, that it is one of the few oldest, least altered buildings in the Parish. Built of three storeys, it has 2 rooms, 1 sitting room, a small kitchen and a bathroom downstairs with 4 bedrooms upstairs and a bedroom and attic on the top floor.

Mr. Albert Griffiths, who was born at Little Overwood when that was a small holding in 1920, inherited Shunesley from his Mother and he and his brother, Robert (Bob), who had actually been born here, came back to live here again in 1973, moving from Woodend Farm. Sadly, Robert has since died but Albert continues to farm the 118 acres with Beef, Sheep and Corn.

Shutley Farm

Shutley farm extends to 65 acres and lies down a long drive, leading off to the right of the road from Hall Orchard to the Nash. The house is of stone and timber, with brick extensions, the oldest part from about 1680 and the newest parts were done in 1959; there are 5 bedrooms, 2 bathrooms, 2 sitting rooms, and 2 kitchens.

The farm has been in the Link family for over 200 years but is currently owned by Brian Link and his Mother, Frances (nee Hinton) Link, who came here, from Buckeridge Rock, after her marriage to her husband, Allan, in 1936. Sadly Allan died in 1987, and then their son, Brian, who had been a partner as from 1970, became joint owner with Frances, who lives here with him and her daughter-in-law.

Brian married Carol (nee Pain) from Cleobury Mortimer, in 1978 and they have two children:- Edward, who is 18 years old, and attends Walford College of Agriculture, and - Katherine, 15, who goes to Lacon Childe School in Cleobury Mortimer.

Six Ashes Riding Centre

The Six Ashes Riding Centre, which was formerly known as Wyre Farm Bungalow, lies on the left side of the Bridgnorth-Cleobury Mortimer road about 100 metres below the Six Ashes crossroads. Built of brick around 1940, the house consists of 3 bedrooms, a bathroom, a sitting room and kitchen.

In 1996, Charles Maurice Lockyer, who was born in Harrow, Middlesex, and his wife, Lorraine Anne, (nee Holden), born in Bolton, Lancs, bought the place and moved here from Stourport on Severn. Charles presently works as the Health and Safety Officer at the Pioneer Centre, while Lorraine is the Proprietor and Instructor of the Riding School which she has developed as diversification on the 20 acres of land; they were married in Portsmouth in 1985 and have 2 children: - Stephanie Rachel, who is 9 years old, and - Jenna Karin, $7^1/_2$ years, who both go to the C.of E. School at Bayton.

Stepple Hall

Stepple Hall, one of the thirteen listed Grade II buildings in the Parish, has been built over three periods, the oldest part being the Tudor half-timbering which probably dates from the early 1600s though there could well have been an earlier building on the site as the name appears in the Domesday Book.

A Queen Anne house was added to the west side and there is a further Georgian extension on the north side.

Paul John Harbach, who is a Chartered Accountant, born in Hagley, married Heather, (nee Bryan), at St. Mary's Church, Neen Savage, in 1977 and they bought Stepple and came to live here, from Cleobury Mortimer, in 1986, to share the accommodation with her parents, John and Patricia Mary (nee Adey) Bryan, who had been living in the School House. Sadly, John died in January 1999, but Pat, a retired Schoolteacher, still lives in their part of the house using 2 of the 9 bedrooms, a sitting- cum-dining room and sharing the kitchen; the house also has 3 bathrooms, a ballroom, dining room, 3 reception rooms, front and back hall, 2 pantries and cellars. Pat and John had a second daughter, Melanie, who was married to John Gardiner and emigrated to Canada, where, though now divorced, she still lives in Burlington, Ontario with her two children, Laura, aged 17, and Andrew who is $14^{1}/_{2}$ years old.

Paul and Heather Harbach have two sons: - James Paul, who is 17 years old and - Edward Geoffrey, 15, who both go to Shrewsbury School.

Stepple Hall Farm of 180 acres, was sold off in the 1980s and bought by Dick Evans of Curdale, though the buildings were retained by the then owner,

Christopher Woodward. However, Paul and Heather Harbach, when they bought the house, also purchased the nearest buildings along with four and a half acres, and, about ten years ago, they bought the rest of them, which included a listed Tythe Barn.

Stepple Lodge

In October 1996, Mike John Lambert, born in Preston, Lancs in 1963, with his wife, Debbie Kim (nee Harris), born in Cuckfield, Sussex in 1968, bought Stepple Lodge, as joint owners, and moved here from Kidderminster. Mike is Head of Call Centre Operations (National Power) and Debbie is Manager of the Academic Quality Unit, University College, Worcester; they were married in Selsey, Sussex in 1992 and have a daughter, Catherine Emma, known as Katie, aged 1 year.

Formerly known as Stepple Hall Lodge, this was originally two stone cottages, built approximately 150 years ago, then knocked into one. Upstairs, there are 3 bedrooms with a bathroom, toilet and landing while downstairs are a kitchen, dining room, sitting room and porch. Since coming here, the Lambert's have redecorated the inside, including quarry tiling the kitchen and porch floors and exposing the timber floor in the bedroom. Outside, they have re-fenced the property, removing a large conifer hedge, which they have replaced with a mixed hedge, and re-roofed, and put a new floor in, the stable; they have also re-designed the garden. Though not a farm, they keep 4 breeds of poultry: Sebright, Silkie and Cochin Chickens with Brecon Buff Geese and "a goat called Monica"!

Stone House

Stone House, which stands on the right by the cross roads up from the ford, was built of stone and half-timbering in 1626 and was the farmhouse on a 60 acre farm owned by Hopton Estates, but the farm was sold off in the late 80s and Derek Winslow bought the house and came here from Medenham, near Marlow, in 1991, with his wife, Janet (nee Groves). The house consists of 4 bedrooms, 2 bathrooms, 2 staircases, 2 sitting rooms, 1 morning room, 1 study, a kitchen, hall and a cloakroom.

Derek Winslow was born in Lancashire, and was the Principal of U.W.I.C. before retirement, and Janet, who was born in Birmingham, was a teacher; they were married in the Parish Church of St. Nicholas at King's Norton in 1960, and have two grown-up children: - Richard, who lives in the Thames Valley, and - Gillian, who lives in Lincoln with her husband and two children.

There are about 5 acres of ground with the property and the Winslows' have done a great job towards making a small wood, having planted some 1,000 native trees of oak, ash, wild cherry, larch, and small leaved lime on part of the acreage, along with an avenue of pear. Developing the garden, as well as conserving the house, are "on-going pursuits!"

Stonehouse Barns

These buildings were originally a barn and milking parlour belonging to Stonehouse Farm and were converted into 3 dwellings in 1984. They are the first buildings on the left of the road down to the ford from Stonehouse.

No.1. is the original barn, half-timbered with brick and stone, which now consists of a kitchen, utility room, dining room, living room, hallway, cloakroom, and snooker room, with 4 bedrooms, (2 en-suites) and a bathroom. Alan John Bates bought Stonehouse Barns and came to live here in January 1996 from the Barn House, Catherton; he is a builder, who was born in Smethwick as was his wife Jacqueline, (nee Price) and they were married there in 1962; sadly, she has since died. They had 4 children:-

– Paul Alan, a Builder, married to Megan and they live in Hay-on-Wye with their 5 children - Rhianne, Carys, Jack, Bethany and Kieran.
– Mia, who is a Dancing Teacher, living in Oldbury, Warley, married to David Gibbs with 3 children - Daniella, Cassie and Trudie.
– Michael John. See No. 3
– David Jonathon, also a Builder, living in Kidderminster with his wife, Lorina, and their 2 children - Sophie and Daniel.

No.2. was part of the original milking parlour and is currently unoccupied.

No.3. was also previously the milking parlour and, built of brick, it now contains a kitchen, sitting room, study, and entrance hall with 4 bedrooms and 2 bathrooms. Michael John Bates, a Builder, who was born in Smethwick, moved here from Oldbury in January 1997 with his wife, Tina

Elaine, (nee Martin) who was born in Birmingham. They were married in Holy Trinity Church, Smethwick in June, 1988 and have 3 children: - Mathew John, aged 10, - Natalie Olivia, who is 8 years old, and they are both at school, and - Joshua Francis, who is 2 years old.

The Bungalow, Upper Elcott

The Bungalow, Upper Elcott, is the first building on the left taking the Stottesdon Road from Six Ashes. Brick built in 1979, it replaced the 17th Century half brick and timbered farmhouse which fell into disrepair, became derelict, was condemned and finally demolished. The Bungalow consists of 3 bedrooms, a sitting room, kitchen and bathroom; a double garage was erected on adjacent land in 1999, and work is still going on to improve the garden etc.

Charles Arthur Skellern, born in Cleobury Mortimer, and his wife, Emily Selina, (nee Carpenter) who was born in Menith Wood, came from Redthorne Dairy to farm the 104 acres of Upper Elcott, in 1946. They had three children: - Tony, who married Sue Gittens and had 3 children, Elizabeth, Michael and Marie, was divorced and now lives in Cleobury with Jo Reid by whom he has had Gareth, Troy, Matt and Jade. - Sue, married to Will Redman, who lives in Eardington with their son Luke, aged 6, and daughter Christina, aged 4. and - Paul, who works at Purslow's Coal Merchant in Cleobury Mortimer where he lives with his son James. Emily also has 3 great grandchildren, Sophie, Ben and Emma, who are the children of Elizabeth.

When Charles retired, the farm was sold, though 14 acres have been retained on which calves, for bringing on, and sheep are kept.

The Cottage, Wyre Common

For many years, this was the house of the Headmasters of the various schools, or other forms of education on the site of the present Pioneer Centre and was known as "Coventry Mead" when Mr. George Parker was Headmaster at the City of Coventry School. Since then it has been sold off the site and Andrew Monk, who was born in Kent, bought it with his wife, Tracy Jane (nee Lindquist), born in Staffordshire, and they moved here from Redditch in July 1999; they were married in Thailand in 1993 and both work in the Construction Industry.

Built of stone, the cottage is thought to be at least 300 years old and has 2 bedrooms, a bathroom, sitting room, a study and a kitchen; the Monks' have recently added a double garage.

The Lodge

Known formerly as No 2 Wyre Farm Bungalow, the Lodge was built in 1947, as temporary accommodation for workers on the Wales to Birmingham water pipe line; originally timber framed with asbestos and felt cladding, a brick skin was added in 1976 and it now consists of 4 bedrooms, a lounge, dining room and kitchen.

It was bought by Steven Barlow, born in Kinver, and Amanda Salt, who was born in Blakedown, and they moved here from Kidderminster in 1997; they have one son, Stephen, aged 10 years, who attends Severndale School, Shrewsbury. As they both have Nursing backgrounds, they take care of children, from all over the country, aged from 0 - 12 years, who are unable to remain with their family of origin, and they are currently looking after George, aged 5^1/$_2$ years. They also run a wheel-chair accessible Minibus Service. Amanda and Steven are also busy with general improvements to, and the updating and modernising of, the Lodge, which is now to be known as "Harvest Edge".

The Nash

The Nash, set to the right above the Cleobury Mortimer to Hall Orchard Road, just above the Baveney crossroads, is a brick and stone building dating back at least 200 years. An old cow shed was joined to the house and converted to a cottage of 2 bedrooms, a bathroom, reception room, and kitchen and the house has 5 bedrooms, a bathroom, 3 reception rooms, kitchen and downstairs toilet.

Anthony Leonard Smith, who was born in Beckenham, Kent, and is a Commercial Property Consultant married Jane Margaret, (nee De Courcy Thompson), born in Nottingham, in Harpenden, in 1967, and they bought the Nash in 1994, moving here from Balsall Common. They have two grown-up children: - Helen Wendy, a Customer Services Assistant, living in Goudhurst, Kent, and - Gayle Jacqueline, a Hotel Conference and Banqueting Co-ordinator, who married Adam Joliffe in 1994, and they are currently living in Cheswick Green, Solihull.

The Old Barn

The Old Barn, as its name implies, was a stone and half-timbered barn, on Lower Neen Farm, which was sold off for conversion to a dwelling and currently consists of 3 bedrooms, and a bathroom upstairs and a kitchen, dining room and lounge downstairs, with plans to convert the rest to a utility room, another bathroom, a sitting room and another bedroom.

Before work started

Richard Anthony Price, born in Farlow, and his wife, Alison Louise, (nee Drennan), born in Bristol, were married in St Mary's, Cleobury Mortimer in 1992 and, having bought the Old Barn, moved here in 1996; they have two children: - James Michael, who is six years old and goes to Cleobury Mortimer Primary School and - Hayden Richard, who was born on the 27th July 1998. Richard is a self-employed Contractor and has a brother, Andrew, who lives in Bury Cottage and his Mother is living at Wood-End.

The Old Forge, Baveney Wood

The Old Forge, which lies on the right up the unsealed lane to Baveney Wood, leading to the left off the Cleobury Mortimer - Bridgnorth road, is a stone built house, thought to be about 300 years old, with 3 acres of ground. The house has 3 bedrooms, 2 bathrooms, a lounge, dining room, kitchen and office, with a front porch added; there are also outbuildings and a double garage.

It was bought in 1983 by Andrew Michael Vanderhook, who was born in Brighton, in 1940, and is a retired Oil Company Senior Executive. His wife, Jennifer Elizabeth, (nee White), was born in Norwich, in 1938 and they married at Helmingham, Suffolk in 1963. They moved here from Swanmore in Hampshire and have 2 grown up children: - Francis Katherine, married to Peter Whitehead with 2 children, Oliver Jack and Sophie Naomi, and they live in Headly Down, Hampshire, and - David Allan, a Company Director, living in London and married to Jo (nee MacDonald).

Andy and Jenny have had a Privy converted into an office, a second greenhouse constructed, along with a patio area, and additional garden walls have been built. All hedges are now laid and a conservation area of about 2 acres, including ponds, has been developed for wildflowers, birds and buttefflies.

The Old Vicarage

The Old Vicarage, as it is now known, stands off the road opposite to St. Mary's Church, and, built around 1755, as the Vicarage for the Parish, remained as such until 1983, when the incumbent, the Revd. Roger Heywood-Waddington, moved to St Michael's, near Tenbury Wells, and the house was sold to Mr and Mrs. Michael Ward. The house had to be re-roofed using lead, the wiring had to be re-done and, amongst other renovations, a new and bigger kitchen was made, so the house now consists of 3 bathrooms, 5 bedrooms and a dressing room upstairs with a drawing room, dining room, study and hallway with the new kitchen downstairs.

There are still outbuildings of a double garage, coal/wood store and potting shed etc. Many of the trees that were in the garden blew down in the storm of 1997, and currently the walled garden is being converted from fruit and vegetables to a pleasure garden. Meanwhile the pool has been re-done.

In 1963, Michael John Ward, who was born in Wolverly, married Judith Ann (nee Pudner), born in Kidderminster, and they moved here from Bewdley with their two daughters: - Charlotte, who now works in Worcester University and lives in the Vicarage Cottage, and - Emily, a Designer, living and working in Manchester. Michael was an Opthalmic Optician, working in Stourport, before retiring in 1997.

The Parish Hall

With the closure of the City of Coventry School, the Parish had no meeting place and the community seemed to be disintegrating; it was hoped that with the building of a Parish Hall, there would be a real centre in which people could meet and where events could take place to the benefit of both Parishioners and the Church. At a Public Meeting, a vote was taken in favour of going ahead, the Glebe land for the Parish Hall was bought from the Diocesan Church and there ensued a lot of fundraising events throughout the Parish, to add to grants from the District and County Councils towards the total cost of £30,000

Finally, the money, £5,000, was raised, the grants awarded and work began on the building of the Parish Hall in 1985. Bishop Mark Woods, Suffragan Bishop of Ludlow, performed the opening ceremony on July 12th, 1986. The

As on opening day, July 12 1986

Hall consists of a lobby, kitchen, the Hall itself and toilets; next year it is planned to begin work on making more cupboard space for storage and the toilets more accessible for the disabled. Meanwhile, the Hall is constantly in use as a venue for private parties, wedding receptions, funeral wakes and further fundraising events, as well as being in regular use for Parish Council and W.I. Meetings, Whist Drives and the Christmas Concert. The Car Park was tarmaced in 1995, and has proved a real boon for both church-goers and Parish Hall events.

Upper Baveney Farmhouse

Upper Baveney Farmhouse is found at the top of the lane, which goes off to the left from the Old School to Baveney House road. Thought to be about 300 years old, it is built of stone with an end gable of brick and a pantile roof from a later date. The house has 4 bedrooms, bathroom, drawing room, kitchen, scullery and a hall.

In June, 1999, Robert Andrew Huntsman Marston-Smedley and his wife, Victoria Claudia Marcia, (nee Knight) bought Upper Baveney and came here from Bayton. Robert was born in Birmingham in 1962 and he is a tree stump grinder and makes Pet Fences, while Victoria was born in Detmold, Germany in 1967 and does Recruitment, (a back-up for finding people work); they were married at Bramley in 1996.

Vicarage Cottage

It is not known for sure whether the brick built Vicarage Cottage was ever integral with the Vicarage, but it is known that, after the Second World War, much of the Servants Quarters of the Vicarage were demolished and what became the Cottage was divided off and used as a separate residence for the Verger and subsequently the Organist. The Cottage was bought by Michael and Judy Ward, along with the Old Vicarage, in 1983 and consists of 3 bedrooms, a bathroom, sitting room and an office.

Currently, Charlotte Ward, elder daughter of Judy and Michael, who works at Worcester University, is living here with Paul Krivocite, from Stourport on Severn.

Walfords Bridge Cottage

Walfords Bridge Cottage, built of stone and brick some 300 years ago, stands at the end of the track (Blackberry Lane) leading off to the right between the Church and Lower Neen Farm; it was originally a mill and then became a blacksmith's shop before being converted into two cottages. Mr. and Mrs. John Bills, parents of the present owner, bought the cottages, in 1962, and they were knocked into one, using stone from some pigsties and outhouses to make the fireplaces and turning the stables into a laundry with other rooms added on.

In 1989, a complete renovation was carried out so that, presently, the house consists of 5 bedrooms, two bathrooms, kitchen, living room, toy room, dining room and a laundry with 2 utility rooms.

Daniel Benjamin Bills, an Engineer, was born in Norton, Stourbridge in 1962, and is the second son of Mr and Mrs John Bills, so has lived here most of his life; in 1988, he married Caroline Suzanne (nee Ashlee), who was born in Montreal, Canada, and is a Special Needs Assistant, and she moved in with Daniel to live here, after the renovations were completed, in 1990. They have 5 sons: - Adam James, born in August 1985 and now in year 10 at Lacon Childe School, - George Oliver, who was born in September 1988, is also there in year 7, - Jack Daniel, 10 years old this April, is in year 5 at Cleobury Primary School - Joseph William, born in June, 1991, is there in year 4, and - Samuel Benjamin, who was born in July 1994, is in year 1, also at Cleobury Primary School.

Mr. and Mrs. John Bills also bought **WEIR COTTAGES** but these have now fallen into ruin.

Wall Town

The Haywood family have owned Wall Town Farm for many years and David Haywood has lived here all his life. He now lives here with his second wife, Elizabeth, (nee Prosser) who was born in Hereford and their daughter, Kerry Ann, aged 9 years. David had 3 daughters, now grown-up, by his first marriage, Elizabeth, Katherine and Joanna, and Elizabeth had 3 daughters, also now grown-up, by her first husband, Peter Plant, and they are Sophia, Samantha and Charlotte. David is a Member of Kinlet Parish Council and he and Elizabeth were married in December 1999. Elizabeth works as a Kitchen Cook at the Primary School in Cleobury Mortimer.

The house consists of 6 bedrooms, all with showers en-suite, a bathroom, 2 sitting rooms, a dining room, kitchen and cellars. Currently the house is up for sale and the family will be moving once it is sold. The farm extends to 300 acres. producing potatoes, cereals and sheep.

Wall Town Cottages

Brick built as farmworkers cottages in 1948, these cottages stand on the left of the Cleobury Mortimer to Kinlet road about 100 yards before the entrance to Wall Town Farm.

Number 1 Wall Town Cottages has been taken on by Ronald Smith, and his wife, Christine (nee Cotton) who were both born in Tipton. They were married in West Bromwich in 1972 and have 2 children: Elizabeth who is 14 and goes to Lacon Childe School in Cleobury Mortimer, and William, aged 7 years old, who goes to Kinlet, C. of E. School. Ron does Domestic Appliance Repairs and Christine is a Carpet Designer.

They moved here from Kidderminster in 1996 and have since installed double glazing and central heating in the house, and added an extra bathroom, a kitchen and a conservatory so that now the house consists of 3 bedrooms, 2 bathrooms, sitting room, dining room, kitchen and conservatory; a garage has also been built.

Number 2 Wall Town Cottages was bought by Alan Keith Newton, who was born in Cradley Heath and his wife, Christine Ann, (nee Williams) of Halesowen, and they moved here in 1999, from Halesowen; he is a Cabaret Vocalist and she is a Costume Maker. They were married at St Peter's Church in Cradley in 1968 and have two children: - Anna Louise, who is attending King Edward VI College, and - Claire Joanne, married to Stuart Pell, living in Halesowen with their 6 month old daughter, Rebekah May.

The Newtons are carrying out a complete refurbishment to the whole house including new windows, central heating, new kitchen etc. A bedroom has been converted to a new bathroom upstairs and the old bathroom downstairs has been made into a study/3rd bedroom. An en-suite bathroom is being made for the main bedroom, so that the house will consist of a kitchen, lounge and study/bedroom downstairs, with 2 bedrooms and 2 bathrooms upstairs.

Wall Town House

Wall Town House, which lies to the right, off the Cleobury Mortimer to Bridgnorth road, just before the drive up to Cleobury Lodge, was built of brick in 1938. It has a kitchen, dining room, lounge, hall, sun room, 3 bedrooms and a bathroom.

In 1968, George Haywood and his wife, Mary, (nee Wells), whom he married at Arley in September 1939, came to live here when he retired from farming at Wall Town Farm. Sadly, George died in December 1998. They had three children: - John, who farms at Lower Baveney, - David, who has Wall Town Farm, and - Rosemary, married to Lewis Williamson, living in Eardington,

Bridgnorth with their three children, Guy, Clare and Mark. Mary also has her grandson, George, living at Cleobury Lodge Barn, with her three great granchildren: John, Guy and Sarah.

Woodbine Cottage, Baveney Wood

Originally, this cottage was a small stone built "two up and two down" type, probably built about 250 years ago, but it has been enlarged and now consists of 3 bedrooms and a bathroom upstairs, and a kitchen, lounge, dining room and toilet downstairs, with the extensions rendered; the main alterations were done in 1984 but further extensions and alterations are on-going. It stands on the right down a right hand fork coming down Baveney Common Lane.

In May, 1990 Ian Beddows, born in Burton on Trent, with his wife, Rachel (nee Miles), born in Birmingham, moved here from Cleobury Mortimer. Mr. Beddows is a Teacher at Pensnett School of Technology and Mrs. Beddows teaches at Cleobury Mortimer Primary School. They married in Birmingham is 1986 and have two children: - Gemma Louise, aged 7, attending Cleobury Mortimer Primary School and - William Jack, aged 3, who goes to Cleobury Mortimer Nursery.

Woodcock Cottage

Woodcock Cottage is at the end of a lane leading off to the right from the drive up to Cleobury Lodge; originally, like Woodbine Cottage, it was a small stone built "two up and two down" cottage but a brick extension was added and it now consists of a lounge, dining room, kitchen, 3 bedrooms and a bathroom.

In 1967, Maurice Robert John Maxwell, who was born in Tenbury Wells, married Irene Mary (nee Birch), born in Bewdley, and they came here as tenants and then bought the cottage in 1971. They had one son, Mark, who tragically died in January, 1995. Presently Maurice is working as a shop assistant in Mumford's, Cleobury Mortimer, and Irene works on a farm.

Wood-End Farm, Bagginswood

The house for Wood-End Farm probably dates from 1780 and was built of bricks, possibly made at the neighbouring farm of Shunesley; the hollows, from which the local clay for the bricks was extracted, can still be seen on the farm at Wood-End. It consists of 3 bedrooms, 2 reception rooms, a kitchen and bathroom. It lies on the edge of the Parish.

Ivor Price, and his wife, Evelyn Mary (nee Link), who was born in Farlow, came here in 1975 from Upper House, Kinlet. They were married in Farlow in 1957 and there are 4 grown up children: - Linda, who is a teacher, - Andrew, married to Jill (nee Cope), from Cleobury Mortimer, lives at Bury Cottage with their two sons, Benjamin, aged 9, and William, 7, and one daughter, Sophie, 1½ years old; - Heather, an Accountant, married to Stephen Choate, living in Epsom, Surrey with two daughters, Catherine, aged 3, and Laura, whose second birthday is January 3rd, 2000; and - Richard who, with his wife Alison, (nee Drennan) from Cleobury Mortimer, lives at the "Old Barn", with their two sons, James, aged 5 and Hayden, 1½.

Sadly, suddenly and unexpectedly, Ivor died in January 1997 but Evelyn continues to rent and farm the 70 acre farm, with her son Andrew, running 160 breeding ewes and growing beans and barley.

Wyre Bungalow, Wyre Common

Wyre Bugalow was built, by a Mr. Bayliss, in 1968 to house his mother and housekeeper, but it was bought in 1978, a year after he and his wife Thelma, born in Yorkshire, moved to Wyre Cottage, by John Norman Westbrook Hardy, who was born in Southampton of the Westbrook family of Droxford in Hampshire. He was a Methodist Minister, serving in Swaledale for some years, but left the Ministry to get a degree in psychology and social sciences at Durham University; after working in the industrial side of personnel management he moved to the educational side becoming a lecturer in industrial relations at Bilston College of Further Education, Wolverhampton. Sadly, Thelma died in July, 1996 while they were on holiday and, now retired, John has become an author and has had two books published - "The Hidden Side of Swaledale" and, this year, "The Life and Times of James Natrass - The Reluctant Pilgrim". In the course of his research for these books, he has walked extensively on the moors and had to go down many of the old, and not very safe, lead mines where he gained a wealth of information on what life might have been like for the miners and people of Swaledale between 1752 and 1822, when the lead mining activity was at its peak - the times encompassed in his books.

John and Thelma Hardy also own Wyre Common, which they bought in 1978, the rights having lapsed, planning to preserve it in its natural state. They have 2 sons: Christopher, (see Wyre Cottage) and Nicholas.

Wyre Common Cottage

To be found just about opposite the entrance to the Pioneer Centre, Wyre Common Cottage, which was known for many years as Walksman Cottage, was built of brick in the 1920s to house the local overseer or "walksman" for the water supply line from Elan Valley to Birmingham. It now consists of 3 bedrooms, bathroom, sitting room, dining room and kitchen.

In 1983, Bernard Thomas Williams, who was born in Elton, moved here with his wife, June Margaret, (nee Bate), from Downton where they were married in 1958. They have two grown up children:- Julie, who is a secretary and - Glyn, a mechanic. Bernard is now retired but he was a Walksman's Helper and his wife is a Cleaner.

Wyre Cottage, Wyre Common

Lying to the right of the road down to the Golf Course, this cottage, built of stone in the 16th century, was originally only 4 small rooms, but over the years it has had extensions built on and now consists of a large sitting room, galleried hall, cloakroom and boiler house downstairs with 3 bedrooms and a bathroom upstairs.

Christopher John Hardy, who was born in Macclesfield, came to live here in 1977 with his parents, (see Wyre Bungalow, Wyre Common). After graduating in Physics at Aston University in Birmingham, he became a Teacher and lived in Wolleston, West Midlands; in 1985, he married Julie Dawn Link, who was born in Kidderminster, at Farlow Church and they lived in Newport, Shropshire before coming back to Wyre Cottage. They have two children; Lindsey Dawn, aged 8 years old and Andrew John, who is 2 years old, both attending Cleobury Mortimer Primary School.

Wyre Farm

Wyre Farm is the first farm down a long track on the left of the road from Six Ashes towards the Pioneer Centre. The house was built of stone in the 18th century, is 4 storeys high and has lots of old oak and ships timbers; it consists of 4 bedrooms, sitting room, dining room, kitchen, pantries and a cellar.

Richard Skellern has lived here all his life; since the death of his father, Jim Skellern, in 1984 and of his mother, Edwina, in 1989, Richard has been farming the 96 acre farm himself producing beef, sheep and corn. His cousin, Charlie Skellern lives at Upper Elcott.

Yew Tree Cottage, Baveney Wood

Roger Jones, a builder, who was born in Blackheath, bought Yew Tree Cottage and, moving from Bromsgrove, came to live here in 1981 with his wife Margaret, who sadly died in 1998. They were married at St. Mary's, Halesowen in 1968 and there are two grown-up children: - Claire, a Teacher at North London University, who is married to Simon Crawley and lives in Hemel Hempstead with their son, Scott Samuel; and - Helen, who lives in Sheffield and is a Teacher at Sheffield University.

The 250 year old brick and stone built house has been completely converted and now consists of 3 reception rooms, a kitchen, 2 bathrooms and 3 bedrooms. Yew Tree Cottage stands on the right above Rose Cottage, up the Baveney Common Lane from the Cleobury Motimer to Kinlet road.

Yew Tree Farm

Yew Tree Farm stands on the right of Baveney Common Lane, entering off the Kinlet to Stottesdon road. Mr. and Mrs. Reginald Davis are presently living here.

APPENDIX I

LISTED BUILDINGS

GRADE II

Barn, Elcott.
Lower Elcott.
Nethercott Cottage.
Stonehouse.
Walltown Farmhouse.

Cart Shed, Stepple.
Lower Neen Farmhouse
Overwood Farmhouse.
Stepple Hall.

Detton Mill House.
Nethercott Farmhouse
Reaside Farmhouse.
The Old Vicarage.

GRADE 11*

St. Mary's Church   Detton Hall

APPENDIX II

ORGANISATIONS

THE PARISH COUNCIL

Chairman:	Mr. Eric C. Ratcliff.	(Detton Hall)
Vice-Chairman:	Mrs. Pat Bryan.	(Stepple Hall)
	Mr. George Haywood.	(Cleobury Lodge Barn)
	Mr. Jim Hulme.	(Lower Neen Farm)
	Mr. Raymond Pearce.	(Bank Top Farm)
	Mr. Michael Tomkinson.	(Nethercott Farm)
	Mr. Philip Turner.	(Melbury)
Clerk to the Parish Council:	Mr. David Shackleton.	(Hillside)

THE PAROCHIAL CHURCH COUNCIL

Chairman:	The Revd. Preb. Robert Horsfield.	(The Vicarage, Cleobury Mortimer)
Curate:	Revd. Andy Sewell.	(Glebe House, Cleobury Mortimer)
Lay Chairman:	Mr. John Griffiths.	(Beneliza, Overwood Farm)
Church Wardens:	Mr. John Haywood.	(Baveney House, Lower Baveney)
	Mrs. Pat Bryan.	(Stepple Hall)
Secretary:	Mrs. Barbara Rowland.	(Orchard End, Cleobury Mortimer)
Treasurer:	Mrs. Sue Del Mar.	(Cleobury Lodge)
Members:	Mr. Bryan Link.	(Shutley)
	Mr. David Shackleton,	Organist (Hillside)
	Mr. Anthony Smith.	(The Nash)
	Mrs. Jane Tomkinson.	(Reaside)
	Mrs. Jill Williams.	(The Cottage, Coombe Farm)

EDWARDS & HINCKESMAN FOUNDATION

Trustees:		
Chairman:	Mr. Eric Ratcliff.	(Detton Hall)
	Mr. Philip Engleheart.	(Kinlet Hall)
	The Revd. Preb. Robert Horsfield.	(The Vicarage, Cleobury Mortimer)
	Mr. John Griffiths.	(Beneliza, Overwood Farm)
	Mr. Derek Winslow.	(Stonehouse)
Clerk to the Trustees:	Mr. David Shackleton.	(Hillside)

THE VITAL LINK

Editorial Board Members:	John and Sue Del Mar (Cleobury Lodge)
	Paul and Angela Flowers (Dinmoor)
	Geoff Massey (Cleobury Mortimer)
	Brenda Weaver (Cleobury Mortimer)
Treasurer:	Christine Haywood (Baveney House)
Editor-in-Chief:	Elisabeth Ratcliff (Detton Hall)

PARISH HALL COMMITTEE

Chairman:	Mrs. Clare Ratcliff.	(Little Detton)
Secretary:	Mrs. Angela Flowers.	(Dinmoor)
Treasurer:	Mrs. Carol Link.	(Shutley Farm)
	Mrs. Pat Bryan.	(Stepple Hall)
	Mrs. Jan Hallett.	(Detton Mill House)
	Mrs. Annie Pearce.	(Bank Top Farm)
	Mr. Philip Turner.	(Melbury)

MILLENNIUM COMMITTEE

Chairman:	Mrs. Clare Ratcliff.	(Little Detton)
Secretary:	Mrs. Carol Link.	(Shutley Farm)
Treasurer:	Mr. David Shackleton	(Hillside)
	Mr. Geoff Massey.	(Cleobury Mortimer)
	Mrs. Annie Pearce.	(Bank Top Farm)
	Mr. Eric Ratcliff.	(Detton Hall)
	Mrs. Jane Smith.	(The Nash)
	Mr. Michael Tomkinson.	(Nethercott Farm)
	Mrs. Brenda Weaver.	(Cleobury Mortimer)

WOMEN'S INSTITUTE

Officers: President/Sick Visitor:	Mrs. Pat Bryan.	(Stepple Hall)
Vice President:	Mrs. Hazel Wood.	(Cleobury Mortimer)
Secretary:	Mrs. Brenda Weaver.	(Cleobury Mortimer)
Assistant Secretary:	Mrs. J. Cumberworth.	(Cleobury Mortimer)
Treasurer:	Mrs. Angela Flowers.	(Dinmoor)
Committee: Programme Secretary:	Mrs. Margaret Gadd.	(Cleobury Mortimer)
Handicraft/Produce/Outing Secretary:	Mrs. Doreen Sayers.	(Cleobury Mortimer)
Assistant Secretary to Mrs. Sayers:	Mrs. Judy Beckett.	(Upper Bardley, Stottesdon)
Press/Competitions Secretary:	Mrs. Annie Pearce.	(Bank Top Farm)
	Mrs. Jane Smith.	(The Nash)

Members:

Mrs. Meryl Booton.	(Cleobury Mortimer)	Mrs. V. Carter.	(Cleobury Mortimer)
Mrs. Una Dorell.	(Neen House Farm)	Mrs. Barbara Evans.	(Cleobury Mortimer)
Mrs. Pat Hall.	(Cleobury Mortimer)	Mrs. Stroma Lennox.	(Cleobury Mortimer)
Mrs. Janet Maiden.	(Highley)	Mrs. Moira Mould.	(Cleobury Mortimer)
Mrs. Barbara Mumford.	(Cleobury Mortimer)	Mrs. Christine Newton.	(2. Wall Town Cott.)
Mrs. Evelyn Price.	(Wood-End Farm)	Mrs. Elisabeth Ratcliff.	(Detton Hall)
Mrs. Margaret Simpson.	(Cleobury Mortimer)	Mrs. Joy Tomkinson.	(Nethercott Farm)
Mrs. Jenny Vanderhook.	(The Old Forge)	Mrs. Judy Ward.	(The Old Vicarage)

APPENDIX III

SHOPPING LISTS

Metric Weights were made compulsory in January 2000 so this has to be borne in mind when making comparisons!

March 1981	£ p	June 2000	£ p
1/2 lb Tea Bags	72	125 grammes Tea Bags	79
			(Leaf 99p)
1 lb English Bacon	98	500 grammes English Bacon	2.15
1 lb English Cheese	88	500 grammes English Cheese	2.42
1 lb English Butter	86	500 grammes English Butter	98
1 lb Echo Margerine	30	500 grammes Stork Margarine	46
1 lb Sausages	46	500 grammes Sausages	1.29
1 lb Cooked Ham	1.36	500 grammes Cooked Ham @ £6. 8p a kilo	3.06
1 Dozen Eggs	65	1 Dozen Eggs	1.10
Packet Cornflakes	47	500 grammes Cornflakes	99
2 lb Sugar	78	1 Kilogramme Sugar	69
3lb Bag of Flour	47	Bag of Flour	59
Sliced and wrapped Bread	41	Sliced White Bread	62
8 oz Jar Instant Coffee	1.84	8 oz Jar Instant Coffee	3.99
2 Pints Milk	38	1 Litre Milk = 1.136 pts	69
Tin of Salmon	56	Tin of Salmon	2.20
Tin of Pilchards	46	Tin of Pilchards	46
Tin of Beans	16	Tins of Beans vary considerably from 9p to 39p for Heinz	
Tin of Peaches	27	Tin of Peaches	73
Tin of Pears	28	Tin of Pears	81
Tin of Rice Pudding	20	Tin of Rice Pudding	66
Persil Washing Powder	67	Persil Washing Powder	3.11
2 First Class Stamps	28	2 First Class Stamps	52
Total	**13.44**		**28.70**

Prices for the year 2000 were all taken from "Scotties" in Talbot Square. Cleobury Mortimer.